Developing Readers

Planting Seeds for Comprehension

**Primary
Grades K-2**

**25
Comprehension
Strategies**

Developing Readers

Planting Seeds
for
Comprehension

Lessons by
Sarah Eubanks
Geraldine Haggard, D. Ed.

Created by
Pamela Robberson

Contributions from
Mario Campanaro and Jaunee Perry

American Educational Associates Inc.
Allen, Texas

American Educational Associates Inc.
P.O. Box 1751
Allen, Texas 75013-0013

www.AEApub.com

ISBN-978-1-60075-070-0

First Printing, 2007

I Can Learn to Read

There is one thing my family loves,
and that is to read books.
I want to read them by myself,
but it is harder than it looks.

My teacher helps me everyday
She knows I'll learn to read,
so I listen closely to all she says
about the strategies I need.

I have learned my alphabet
And words that I can write.
There are even many words
That I can read by sight.

When I come to an unknown word
I know now know what to do.
I use the words around it
They all give me a clue.

My teacher says to listen closely
To stories I hear and read.
If I take the time to think,
it will help me to succeed.

The who, what, when, why and where,
all make the story's plot.
The order the events happen
tells me an awful lot.

I need to know the main idea,
so details I must find.
They help me with the summary,
if I keep them all in mind.

Authors write to entertain.
Sometimes they make me smile.
Authors write to inform.
They all have a special style.

I have learned so many things.
A good reader I have become.
I read to learn new facts.
I even read for fun!

Now when my family gets their books,
I go to my shelf.
I choose the book I want to read,
and read it by myself.

By Sarah Eubanks

Table of Contents

    Program CD Includes:
    Strategy Definition Charts
    Students Activities
    Graphic Organizers
    Titles for Instruction
    Discussion Wheels
    Mini-lesson Planning Form
    Strategy Lesson Planning Form
    Multiple Strategy Instruction Chart

American Educational Associates Inc.

American Educational Associates, Inc. is dedicated to accelerating learning for all students. Our new research based materials are designed to enhance existing programs. The cohesive, easy to use, step-by-step materials support teachers by providing them with plans for best practices. Through intentional teaching these purposefully designed lessons and materials are proven to quickly accelerate learning for all students.

American Educational Associates, Inc.
Strategies for Reading Success

Established in 1998 American Educational Associates, Inc. is co-owned by Pamela Rudloff Robberson and Mario Campanaro.

About the Authors

Geraldine Haggard, D. Ed. earned her Bachelors and Masters degrees from Texas State College for Women. Her Doctor of Education in Reading was earned at Texas Woman's University. She did an extra year of study at the Ohio State University in Columbus.

She taught for eleven years in small rural schools located in Denton County, Texas. She worked thirty-seven years with Plano Independent School District. During these years she taught 4th grade and Title I Reading. She directed summer programs for Title I and Head Start. As Reading Supervisor, she helped develop the gifted grogram, the dyslexic program, and was Teacher Leader for Reading Recovery. Her university experiences include adjunct teaching at Texas Woman's University, the University of Ohio, East Texas State University, and the University of Texas in Richardson. She has served as an officer for several state and national reading organizations.

After retirement from public school, she served two years as a visiting Professor of Reading at Texas Woman's University. She serves as a facilitator for Journey of Hope, a grief support program for families. Her work includes writing the children's curriculum using children's literature for discussion and activities such as art, music, writing, and crafts. She also serves as chairman of a Retired Teacher's group that provides gifts of four books each year to over a thousand Title I students in the Plano Schools.

Currently she remaines active in state and school curriculum through tutoring in the schools, which provides an atmosphere to remain current in reading research and techniques. She uses her expertise as she serves as a consultant for school districts, and evaluates, edits and writes materials for publishers.

Sarah Eubanks earned her Bachelor Degree in Elementary and Special Education from Texas A&M Commerce and her Masters in Reading and Supervision form Texas A&M College Station. She has received her certification for teaching gifted students and has presented reading workshops at local, regional, state and national levels.

She has taught for twenty-seven years and has taught first grade for twenty-three years. She loves to teach the students with special needs as well as the gifted student. She is currently teaching first grade in Plano Independent School District.

Jaunee Perry graduated from Brigham Young University in 1988 with a B.S. in Elementary Education and has worked as an educator for 18 years. She received certification as a Master Reading Teacher in 2001. Mrs. Perry was trained as a Reading Recovery teacher while working as a Literacy Specialist for the Alpine School District in American Fork, Utah. Currently Mrs. Perry is an Intermediate Literacy Coordinator at Delores E. Thompson Elementary in the Spring Independent School District located in Spring, Texas, where she team teaches a 3rd grade class, provides Language Arts staff development to teachers, and coaches teachers on her campus. Mrs. Perry was a recipient of the Milken National Educator Award in 2004. She is currently pursuing a Masters of Educational Leadership degree through the University of St. Thomas in Houston.

Mario Campanaro began his career in education as a teacher in an inner city high school in Chicago, Illinois. He latter taught reading and social studies to learning disabled high school students before leaving teaching to pursue his passion for the research and publishing of reading materials. He is the founder of Celebration Press and the Argus Education Division. He has held positions in senior management with DLM and The Wright Group. He received his undergraduate degree from The University of Illinois in Champaign, Illinois, his master's degree from Loyola University of Chicago, and he is currently conducting research in reading comprehension and completing his doctoral studies at Texas A & M University - Commerce.

Pamela Rudloff Robberson earned her Bachelor Degree in Elementary Education from the University of Houston in 1977, where she specialized in Reading and Early Childhood. She received training and taught Reading Recovery for twelve years. She taught for twenty-four years in public and private schools where she was an Elementary Literacy and Dyslexia Specialist. She developed curriculum and provided staff development for classroom teachers and summer school. Mrs. Robberson provided private tutoring for fifteen years for elementary students K-5 using the explicit instruction to quickly remediate students to be successful in the classroom. She is currently working as a consultant and representative for American Educational Associates Inc. She develops materials and provides training for classroom and administrators.

Acknowledgments

PDR is the result of current research and classroom teaching. The format includes the four components of comprehension strategy instruction used in the Gradual Release of Responsibility, researched and developed by AEA.
The four phases are:
- teacher modeling
- guided practice
- independent practice
- application of the strategies in real reading

The Program includes the four components that Fielding and Pearson (1994) contend make a successful comprehension program. The four components are:
- large amounts of text reading
- teacher-directed instruction in comprehension strategies
- opportunities for peer and collaborative learning
- occasions for students to talk to a teacher and one another about their responses to reading.

Using AEA's research on gradual release of responsibility, PDR shows teachers how to introduce and demonstrate comprehension strategies and skills at a concrete level using academic language. Lesson plans include activities at varied levels to allow students to practice these skills during listening, conversation, reading and writing.

Cited below is an article for more information on teaching comprehension strategies from the experts:

Fielding, Linda G. and P. David Pearson. "Reading Comprehension: What Works?" Educational Leadership Volume 51, No. 5, February 1994.

Introduction

The work of the master gardener and the teacher of reading comprehension strategies and skills are similar. Each must be familiar with the seeds that need to be planted and when to plant. Each must nurture and cultivate their seeds as they grow and mature into strong plants. The reading teacher is responsible for cultivating readers as they master the use of the reading strategies and skills needed by proficient readers.

The editors and authors of this book looked at 'breaking the soil' before the garden was started. Time was spent investigating what well known researchers have documented about reading strategies and skills found to be helpful to emergent and beginning readers. What strategies begin in kindergarten? Which strategies and skills are more appropriate for grade one? Is there a research base for a teaching sequence of the strategies? The answers to these questions are included in the framework of the guide.

Furthermore, an investigation of the benchmarks, or reading objectives of eight different states was conducted. The strategies and skills included in the Primary Developing Readers Guide are the strategies and skills most commonly taught in kindergarten and grade two across the states surveyed.

Good gardeners know when and where to plant their sends for best results. Reading teachers can feel confident that the strategies included in PDR are important for young readers, regardless of the state in which they live. A correlation of the strategies for kindergarten and first grade indicate that the strategies tested in the intermediate grades are the ones that are mandated for use in read alouds, shared reading, and guided reading in the early grades. The massive amount of independent reading prepares young readers for longer passages and cultivates the fluency needed by successful readers in the later grades.

Master gardeners know the importance of developing a healthy root system in plants. As young children observe modeling and practice the strategy in guided and independent practice, they develop a strong root system that will enable them to orchestrate the strategy as they read and write across the curriculum. The attentive gardener waters and fertilizes the plants daily as needed. As the student and teacher practice the strategy, the teacher observes and provides support when needed. The teacher prompts and encourages the student to transition into independent practice, assuming more and more responsibility for their own growth.

As conditions for the growing plant change each year, so do classroom teachers and leaning environments for student. To accelerate healthy growth it is essential that teachers use common academic language that supports the strategy or skill. As we plan our strategy gardens we want perennial readers that come back year after year without a total replanting. With careful watering and fertilizing of scaffold instruction during modeling and practicing during read alouds, shared reading, guided and independent practice strong, and hardy root structures will enhance continued growth.

The master gardener uses special tools to create a healthy garden. These tools include a shovel, spade fork, rake, gloves, shears, hoe and water can. The reading teacher's basic tools are the student (soil), seed (strategies or skills), shovel or spade (books) to dig into schema (soil) and plant the seed (strategy). The seed is prompted by giving information (watering) by the watchful gardener to accelerate growth. As students grow, the teacher observes and provides needed nourishment to foster growth in reading comprehension.

The garden includes plants at different stages of growth. The reading teacher's master garden plan includes big group, small group, and sometimes, one-on-one teaching. The garden is thoughtfully tended, nurturing the needs of each student, or group of students.

This is a delightful place to be! What a challenge to plant and nurture young readers as they fall in love with books and develop the research based thinking strategies and skills that will enable them to be strong readers as they progress through life. It is exciting to watch the growth of each student is in progress. The editors and authors of this book hope that their work will help make the teachers' task easier and facilitate the existence of a beautiful garden of young readers.

Program Overview
Program Objectives

Kindergarten, first and second grade teachers are approached often by third and fourth grade teachers requesting that they introduce and practice the key strategies such as context clues, main idea, inference, and summary that are tested on standardized test in the intermediate grades. PDR has addressed this need by providing a primary program that introduces these strategies at the concrete level for emergent readers, planting the seeds for comprehension.

Much research has focused on the important question of whether or not comprehension can be taught through explicit instruction. The answer is that the strategies that good readers use to read and make sense of text can and should be taught. AEA believes that comprehension is "taught not caught".

The research on the early development of young readers stresses the importance of early instruction not only in word recognition, but in comprehension. Young readers in the early grades should be taught using explicit instruction on strategies such as summarizing, main idea, predicting, drawing conclusions and monitoring to clarify their understanding.

The purpose of **Primary Developing Readers Planting Seeds for Comprehension (PDR)** is to provide the primary teacher with a research based approach for introducing and practicing essential comprehension strategies, and to guide the student in using these strategies in listening, talking, reading and writing situations.

There are two primary goals of **PDR**: first, to model for students' grade appropriate comprehension strategies and second, to have students practice these strategies through conversation, drawing, and eventually in reading and writing.

To achieve these goals, the program objectives then become:

Student Objectives:

- To develop the student's ability to think and to construct meaning while listening in read aloud and shared reading

- To develop the student's ability to use and apply flexible thinking while problem solving

- To develop the student's ability to construct meaning from a variety of genres

- To provide the students with visual models using graphic organizers to help organize new information

- To provide a model for using academic language and provide a setting to practice key phrases in conversation

Teacher Objectives:

- To provide the teacher with models for teaching comprehension strategies through a gradual release of responsibility

- To provide the teacher with academic language, definitions, and key phrases for comprehension strategies to create consistency and accelerate automaticity in the use of reading strategies K-5

- To provide the teacher with lesson plans for introducing and modeling key comprehension strategies on a concrete level

Program Description

A Research-Based Program

Primary Developing Readers Planting Seeds for Comprehension (PDR) is the result of current research and the classroom teaching experience of the authors. The teaching approach, Gradual Release of Responsibility, is based on the four components of comprehension strategy instruction researched and developed by AEA. See (figure 1) below.

The four steps in this teaching model are:
- teacher modeling
- guided practiced
- independent practice
- application of the strategies in real reading

Fielding and Pearson (1994) go on to say that four additional components are needed:
- large amounts of text reading
- teacher-directed instruction in comprehension strategies
- opportunities for peer and collaborative learning
- occasions for student to talk to a teacher and one another about their responses to reading

Gradual Release of Responsibility

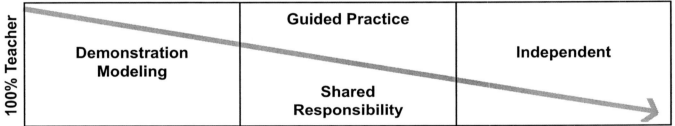

Figure 1. Gradual Release of Responsibility

Implementing PDR

PDR is implemented with minimal expense and can be used with any reading curriculum. The strategies can be modeled with teacher-selected texts containing fiction, nonfiction, poetry, and other genres. Graphic Organizers and charts for student use are provided.

The teacher determines when to implement **PDR**. **PDR** can be used for the entire school year or for intense intervention for a concentrated period, such as a tutoring program or a summer school solution.

The instructional activities have been planned to accommodate the varying time periods available for instruction. The instructional activities developed for **PDR** were designed to be flexible and are presented in sections. These sections can be thought of as "thinkable units" that facilitate time management.

The learning experiences included in **PDR** range from active listening during read-aloud, active participation during shared reading, guided practice in small groups and independent reading and writing. The focus of the reading instruction is modeling and practicing key comprehension strategies in a purposeful and supportive environment.

The gradual release of responsibility model requires that instruction begin with modeling and proceed sequentially through guided practice into independent practice. **PDR** introduces the strategies on a concrete level for early readers.

Please note that some students will progress at a faster pace than others.

Components of PDR

The materials included are:

- 15 Procedural Lessons, Charts and Icons
- 8 Cognitive Strategy Charts and Icons
- 17 Strategy Detailed Lessons Plans
- Definition Charts and Icons for each Strategy
- Academic Language and Key Phrases
- Graphic Organizers for Reproduction
- Suggestions for Centers or Stations for each Strategy
- Strategy Activities for Reproduction
- Suggested Titles for Instructions for each Strategy
- Partnership Discussion Charts

Features and Organization

- **PDR Planting Seeds for Comprehension** begins by preparing the soil for the seeds of comprehension. In order, to plant seeds that grow and flourish it is important to start with fertile soil. The following procedural lessons and thinking strategies prepares the soil for the seeds that will be planted in the primary grades.

- **PDR includes 15 procedural lessons** that provide teachers with structure and routines. This helps create a classroom atmosphere that enables teacher and students to work together as a community of learners. The goal is to create an atmosphere where students become literacy partners: they become active participants during all parts of the gradual release framework, which include reading to, reading with and reading by. These lessons provide the teacher with the structure to establish procedures that soon become routines allowing students to focus on learning.

- **Eight thinking strategies included in PDR** introduce primary students to key strategies during read aloud and shared reading. These strategies develop the students' ability to become active readers who think about the text while reading. Additional Lesson Plans for these strategies are available in our **STOP TO THINK** Program.

- **There are 17 comprehension strategies** containing detailed plans organized for ease of implementation. Teacher-friendly easy to use, scripted plans enable the teacher to confidently and effectively help the student practice strategies. These strategies and skills are introduced, modeled and practiced using teacher selected texts.

- **A Step Beyond** at the end of each Strategy Lesson provides station and extension activities. These activities should not be used until students have been introduced to the skill, and have practiced with the teacher demonstrating an understanding of the strategy. Many of the activities can be used in a station or center for independent practice.

Academic Language

AEA believes in teaching the academic language that students need to become proficient and productive readers. Academic Language can be very confusing for students. Think about math word problems and the language that often gets in the way of students being successful with understanding how to work the problems. Terms such as congruent, parallel, more than, less than, etc. are still a part of essential math academic language. Reading as a content is much the same. Many times students are confused because they don't know certain terms and what they mean. Example: resolution, inference, generalization, traits, etc. AEA knows that students must be taught these terms. Also, they must be taught consistently from grade to grade. For the needy reader, using different terms or multiple terms for strategies can be very confusing. Using consistent terms and definitions allows students to grow as readers from year to year. This allows readers to accelerate by "building on" and "not starting over" each year. Students are scaffolded to use strategies starting at the concrete level and moveing to a more sophisticated level. AEA uses in all our reading programs, state mandated strategies and the academic language that students need to consistently recognize and understand. The terms are introduced during modeling, practiced during guided practice and monitored during independent practice, which prompts, students to use key terms and phrases during discussion and writing.

> *"I want their think-alouds to be genuine, their language precise, their responses thoughtful. I start by helping them format their responses. My goal is to give them a framework for thinking, as well as to help them build a common language for talking about books. For example, when children share their connections, I ask them to begin this way: "When I read these words... it reminded me of..." or "When I saw the picture of... it made me think about..."*
>
> *Miller, Debbie. Reading With Meaning, Teaching in the Primary Grades, p.55 Stenhouse Publishers, 2002*

Key phrases for each strategy are provided on the definition chart. They are introduced, modeled and practiced to prompt students to use academic language when talking and writing about the strategies. Providing key terms and phrases gives a "jump start" for students when practicing strategies.

PDR Key Terms

THINK ALOUD- The teacher thinks aloud during a read aloud session to demonstrate their reading processes and model how they apply comprehension strategies to make sense of the text.

STOPPING POINTS—In order to develop a student's ability to monitor his/her reading **stopping points** are used to control the amount of text he/she reads before being asked to reflect on that text. Initially, the teacher uses stopping points to determine good places in the text to stop and model or practice a strategy. The stopping point offers a good opportunity to demonstrate the strategy in the text. Stopping points can be designated after one paragraph, one page, or several pages. To systematically develop student's ability to understand how to use strategies to examine and develop meaning while reading, teachers model this during read aloud. Later students begin to take over, repeating what they have observed the teacher doing when stopping at stopping points. For best results, teachers should start with shorter amounts of text and gradually increase the length of text. Practicing strategies using small amounts of text, sets up students to be successful by, building self confidence. Decisions about stopping points should gradually be released to the student.

STOP TO TALK—During reading students are asked to **stop to talk**. Sticky notes are used to mark the stopping points. The students stop at the designated stopping points during the reading and turn to a partner to discuss the text. Key phrase are initially given by the teacher to start the students talk, prompting success. Gradually this is released to the students to practice during independent and partnership reading.

STOP TO JOT—As readers become more proficient at stopping to talk about the text using the strategies, they are asked to **stop to jot** during or after reading. In **stop to jot**, students use sticky notes or student response journals to draw or jot down what they are thinking during reading. Talking, drawing or writing during reading requires readers to stay engaged and holds them accountable for monitoring text meaning.

Option: All students are asked to talk about text using the strategies. Depending on developmental level, students draw, dictate or write responses to reading.

K-2 Reading Teachers Want to Know
Strategies for Standardized Testing Included

What state guidelines for standardized text were considered when developing PDR?
AEA reviewed the guidelines of various states, to confirm the importance and consistency of strategies and skills taught to prepare students for standardized tests. Primary Developing Readers has included the strategies and skills found across the country required for standardized testing.

How does PDR fit into state and district curriculums?
PDR is not an add-on; it is an additive resource used with state and district curriculums. **PDR** provides activities for use with district and classroom texts and materials.

Comprehension Strategies

What comprehension strategies are included in PDR?
PDR includes the key comprehension strategies identified by research and recognized in professional reading periodicals, research quarterlies, and recent method guides used in the training of reading teachers.

How do teachers encourage students to "think" as they read?
8 Key Cognitive Strategies are introduced first to provide a framework to enable students to become actively engaged readers that make sense of the text as they read.

Does PDR include strategies for vocabulary development?
PDR contains ideas for modeling and practicing vocabulary strategies that research has identified as helping students develop techniques to locate and understand unknown words.

Audience

What audience is PDR designed for?
PDR is designed for use with emergent and beginning readers. Strategies are introduced using listening, talking and drawing activities, and then moved into reading and writing.

PDR is used as a resource of teaching ideas for the regular classroom teacher, special education, Title 1, and tutorial programs.

How does PDR fit into Early Primary Reading Instruction?
PDR provides ideas and activities for components of early primary programs such as, read aloud, shared reading, guided reading and independent reading.

Does PDR support and accelerate second language learners?
PDR provides learning experiences where students can hear academic language modeled in meaningful context. This is beneficial in helping to build new vocabulary important for ELL students.

Instructional Features

Do strategies need to be introduced in a specific order?
AEA's research based sequence for introducing the strategies is suggested. This can assure success in kindergarten and the later years. Some strategies require the knowledge and use of other strategies. For example: To Retell events the student must be able to sequence events in order.

How does PDR model and prompt students to practice strategies orally?
PDR provides the teacher with academic language in introducing strategy names and key phrases that support student success as they practice strategies through conversation.

Does PDR integrate strategies into expository texts?

PDR includes ideas for integrating strategies into the content area units of study, providing opportunities to practice the strategy in expository texts.

Does PDR include a writing component?

PDR recognizes that reading and writing are parallel and has included writing activities to facilitate both processes to encourage students to write about reading.

Does PDR include organizational tools?

Graphic organizers are included to teach organizational skills by demonstrating and practicing organizing the information provided when using the strategies.

How does PDR support the early readers?

PDR provides icons for easy recognition of strategies and titles of wordless books for early readers.

Does PDR include activities for differentiated instruction?

A Step Beyond, provides station and extension activities for practicing the strategies in real life situations. These activites are great for differentiating instruction.

Teacher Support

How do primary teachers support strategy instruction in K-2 that is consistent with the strategy instruction at the intermediate grades?

PDR provides instruction for the key strategies that is consistent with the Developing Readers at the Intermediate grades. The definitions have been simplified for primary students, and include icons for non-readers.

PDR includes a section called Teacher Talk for each strategy included in the guide. Teacher Talk provides the primary teacher with the strategy definition and key phrases used in the intermediate grades. It also includes the leading research, expectations for reading and writing, and cautions and tips when teaching the strategy to primary students.

How do teachers know which books are appropriate for instruction?

PDR provides a list of titles of books that provide multiple opportunities to practice a strategy in modeling, guided and independent practice.

How do teachers track the strategies taught?

Organizational Charts provide the teacher with a tool to document and monitor when strategies are introduced, modeled and practiced.

Is PDR easy to use?

PDR provides a simple layout including large print and easy to read lesson plans for easy reference while teaching. It includes research and theory, and background information about the strategies and skills. The book is easy to use, the flexible binding facilitates the use of the book during instruction.

PDR was developed by educators currently working in the primary classroom who understand the demands teachers face each day. The teaching ideas included in **PDR** came from their experiences in the classroom and knowledge of children's literature.

Instructional Strategies
17 Comprehension Strategies

Beginning in kindergarten and then continuing through the primary grades, the author found that standards vary from state to state. However, there appears to be 17 comprehension strategies that are common to most state standards and most assessments. These standards are as follows:

Vocabulary

- **Context Clues** – Ability to use words around an underlined word to identify its meaning

- **Best Definition / Multiple Meaning Words** – Ability to use words around an underlined word to understand its meaning and select the best definition

- **Dictionary Entry / Affixes** – Ability to use words around an underlined word to understand its meaning and select the best definition in a dictionary entry – Students also recognize root words and how affixes influence meaning

- **Synonyms / Antonyms** – Ability to use words around an underlined word to understand its meaning and select a word that means the same or its opposite

Story Structure

- **Main Idea / Supporting Details** – Ability to understand what the text or paragraph is mostly about

- **Supporting Details** – Ability to understand the small bits of information stated in the text that help define or give more information about the main idea

- **Text to Support Meaning** – Ability to locate supporting details from the text – The reader locates information directly from the text to answer specific questions.

- **Summary** – Ability to recognize a short paragraph retelling the most important ideas and details in the text

- **Character Traits / Emotions / Motives** – Ability to notice details about how characters look, feel, and act –This helps the reader understand how to identify the characters' feelings and relationships with one another, and begin to question why they do what they do and how they change with the experience.

- **Setting** – Ability to recognize the time and the place the events in the story happen – There may be more than one setting which may influence the lives of the characters and the plot.

- **Plot / Story Problem / Resolution** – Ability to recognize the important events, problems or main conflict, and how the conflict may be solved

- **Order of Important Events** – Ability to recognize and sequence the events in the order in which they happen in the text

Comprehension

- **Cause and Effect** – Why something happens is the **cause**. The **effect** is what happens as a result. Sometimes the author may state the cause or effect in the text, and sometimes it must be inferred

- **Inference** – Ability to take information from the text and what you know to figure out something that is not stated in the text

- **Prediction** – Ability to take information from the text and what you know to make a smart guess about what might happen in the future
- **Drawing Conclusions** – Ability to take information from the text and come to a new understanding
- **Fact and Fantasy** – A **fact** is a statement that can be proven using information from the text. **Fantasy** is something you know can not be true. It is imaginary or make believe.
- **Comparing Story Variants** – Ability to notice how story details are alike and then notice how they are different – The reader may compare the plot, settings, characters, problems, themes, and solutions

Author's Craft

- **Author's Purpose** – Ability to recognize the reason the author is writing – This is based on the text and its purpose. It may be to entertain, to inform, to explain how to do something, or to persuade. The author may have more than one purpose for writing.
- **Genre Format** – Ability to recognize different forms of writing and their features – These include: folk tales, fairy tales, fables, realistic stories, etc.
- **Graphic Organizers** – Ability to use visual diagrams to organize information – Examples: Story Maps, Venn Diagrams, Sequencing, etc.

Key Cognitive Strategies

8 Thinking Strategies

Research has shown that good readers are active and engaged before, during and after reading. Good readers preview the book before reading thinking about the story structure, making predictions, asking questions, connecting to prior knowledge and setting a purpose for reading. They make decisions about the author's purpose, the genre and how to read the text. During reading they continue to make predictions, ask questions and look for answers. Students create a movie or picture in their mind using the author's words and prior knowledge creating a time line of events in their mind. They define new words and search for clues in the text to help them clarify meaning. When focus or meaning is lost, a good reader rereads for confirmation or understanding. After reading, students retell important parts and summarize the author's message.

Listed below are the eight key thinking strategies included in **PDR** that students use to become active, engaged readers . These strategies are introduced in the primary grades through listening to stories read aloud, engaging in discussions during shared reading and small groups, working with partners to read and compare thinking during independent reading. These strategies are not developed and internalize in a few reading sessions. They must be modeled and practiced over an extended period of time. **PDR** introduces these thinking strategies in primary grades in the **STOP TO THINK** Program and continues to practice them during reading and writing in all our reading programs.

Predict	Retell
Ask	Describe
Define	Connect
Reread	Summarize

To introduce, model and practice these strategies, AEA uses **stop to think** and **stop to talk** to think and talk about reading, and **stop to jot** during reading to write about reading.

Instructional Options

Instructional decisions are based on the needs of the students, time restrictions, district reading curriculum and mandated standardized tests. Instruction can be whole group, small group and/or individual settings.

Procedures of Modeling

Before Reading

1. Select the strategy for instruction.

2. Select a familiar text for instruction with a simple story line that provides 3-5 opportunities to model the strategy. Select a text that provides strong, concrete, and obvious examples to model the strategy. (Using familiar text provides knowledge of the vocabulary, and the story line allowing students to concentrate on the strategy being modeled vs. the new story events.)

3. Pre-read the text and select three or five places where you can model the strategy for the students. You must model the strategy a minimum of three times before the students' first attempt to use the strategy.

4. Use sticky notes to write down what you are going to say as you model. Use key phrases to start your talk using concise language to demonstrate what you are thinking. When modeling, demonstrate step by step what you do when you use this strategy, demonstrate the process, problems, ask yourself questions, weigh alternatives, self corrections, and persistence.

5. Model the use of academic language for the strategy. Display the key phrases on the board or chart for students to view as you read.

6. Place one of the sticky notes at the end of the text and ask students to allow the students to 'give it a try' and practice what they have observed you modeling. Support the students by providing the key phrase by saying, ***Turn to your partner and say I predict _____ because _____.*** Allow students just long enough to practice the strategy using the key phrase you have provided. Students take turns turning to their partner and using the key phrase to start their talk. They discuss their thinking and provide evidence from the text. Ask students to 'wind up' their talk. The teacher listens in on talk and asks several students to share.

7. Plan ahead selecting several other simple texts to model this strategy before scaffolding instruction.

During Reading
Teacher's Role

8. Use a visual signal when modeling a strategy to indicate thinking aloud verses reading aloud. Visual signals used when thinking aloud could be: putting the book down, holding the book to your chest and looking up towards the ceiling.

9. Use sticky notes to mark stopping points including the strategy and key phrases for think aloud.

10. Ask students to sit up straight and "Tune In".

Student's Role

11. "Tune In" a term used to remind them to sit up straight and listen with an alert mind.

12. Focus their attention on what the teacher is modeling. They do not raise their hands to make comments or ask questions during modeling.

13. Practice the strategy demonstrated by the teacher with their partner after the reading. The students will 'give it a try'.

During Reading Aloud (Modeling-Think Aloud)

1. Review the title and make predictions about the text.

2. Review the author and discuss whether you have read a book by this author or not.

3. Review the story line, if this is a familiar text.

4. Activate prior knowledge providing a foundation for the reader and setting a purpose for reading. Think Aloud about what you know about the topic.

5. Review the layout of the text. Discuss any text features you notice. Predict whether you think it is a fiction or nonfiction text by looking at the layout. Discuss pictures, captions, subtitles, maps, and graphics if available.

6. Link strategy to previous learning.

7. Explain that you are going to reread the story and this time you will demonstrate (show them) a strategy that proficient readers use when reading.

8. Put key phrases on the board or chart where students can view them. Explain to students that when you use this strategy you will start your talk with one of these key phrases.

9. Read aloud stopping at stopping points (places you have decided are good to demonstrate the strategy) to demonstrate your thinking using key phrases on the prepared sticky notes. Remember to use visual signals when thinking aloud.

10. Think aloud and discuss the process you are going through as you read and use strategies. Model confusion, work out problems, and talk about the small steps you use when using the strategy.

11. Don't ask students questions during the modeling. Don't allow students to ask questions during the modeling.

After Reading

1. Explain that you want the students to give it a try. Students (think aloud) telling their partner what they are thinking using the strategy. Students think aloud to practice what they have observed quickly while it is still fresh on their minds.

2. In order to ensure success, ask students to start their talk with a key phrase you used during the reading, which is also provided on the board. Example: ***Turn to your partner and say I think_____, The character in the story was_____, This reminds me of_____.***

3. To avoid side conversations, allow students only enough time to quickly share their thinking. After a couple of minutes, ask students to wind up their talk.

4. Allow a couple of students or partners to share with the group.

5. This can lead to a reflection time allowing time to discuss how the strategy helps you as a reader to think about and understand the text.

Procedures for Guided Practice

As the teacher has modeled the strategy using think aloud, the students have the opportunities to observe how a skilled reader uses the strategies to construct meaning from the text. After the teacher demonstrates a strategy, the students give it a try, allowing the teacher to observe. It is important to work with students daily in small group settings such as guided reading or strategy lessons to monitor their use of the strategy and growth as readers.

Guided Practice Settings
- Whole group - Mini-lessons
- Whole group – Read Aloud
- Whole group – Shared Reading
- Small group – Instructional Reading Level (similar reading level)
- Small group – Strategy Lessons (similar need)

The types of guided practice instruction listed above, range from whole group to small group instruction. Each of these guided practice settings is intended to be quick and intentional, taking no more than 10-20 minutes to complete.

Mini-lesson – A mini-lesson targets one skill, strategy or concept in a short lesson 10-15 minutes. The teacher names the strategy or skill and then demonstrates the concept with one or more clear examples and invites the students to participate or "give it a try". Students are immediately asked to apply their learning by using linking the strategy or skill in real reading. The teacher reinforces the strategy during share sessions and conferences. Later students share how this strategy or skill helped them when reading. The teacher evaluates students' progress through conferences, records of student observation, reading response journals, etc.

Read Aloud – During read aloud sessions students practice strategies that have been introduced. The teacher selects one to three strategies to practice during the read aloud. The teacher prepares the read aloud texts by using sticky notes to mark good places in the text to practice the specific strategy.
The teacher uses key phrase practiced for the strategy to start the student's discussion. The teacher stops at the stopping point and ask the student to turn to their partner and say, *I wonder _____ because _____.* Allow students just enough time to turn and talk to their partner using the key phrase. Ask students to wind up their talk and ask several students to share. Continue reading to the next stopping point and repeat practicing the strategy selected. (This is a great way to practice multiple strategies).

Shared Reading - A Shared Reading lesson focuses on one instructional strategy and uses a big book and pointer for instruction. During the shared reading demonstration the teacher will think aloud to model the strategy during the reading. Shared Reading uses the same text over several days and the strategy focus can change. Shared Reading text is often used over a five day plan addressing different strategies each day.

Small Group (Guided Reading for Early and Emergent Readers)

1. Teacher introduces the book and makes predictions or asks, *I wonder _____*, questions during the book walk before reading.
2. Teacher introduces new vocabulary words before reading.
3. Students read entire text orally as the teacher observes and coaches as needed.
4. Teacher develops the teaching point(s) from reading and presents to the group.
5. At the end of the lesson quickly attend to a comprehension strategy that has been introduced and modeled. Options: Retell the story after rereading, Define new words, discuss the Characters, Summarize the story, etc.
6. The teacher may choose to model a strategy after the guided reading lesson. Example: The teacher may summarize the text. The teacher names the strategy and then model the strategy.
7. The teacher may ask the students to turn to their partner and practice the strategy. The teacher supports the students by providing the key phrase and asking the students to turn to their partner and discuss the strategy.
8. After the guided reading session, the student may reread the text with a partner and discuss.

Small Group (Guided Reading for Fluent Readers)

1. Pass out new books and one sticky note for each student.
2. Introduce the book and ask students to mark the first stopping points with sticky notes. Teacher selects the stopping point using a small amount of text and provides a good place to practice the strategy. Stopping points can be 1-2 pages or several paragraphs. Ask students to place their sticky notes at the stopping point.
3. The teacher introduces new vocabulary if necessary.
4. The teacher asks the student to read to the stopping point and then turn to their partner and practice the strategy selected.
5. Students read silently or orally to the stopping point.
6. Students stop at the stopping point and turn to their partner and using a key phrase practice the strategy the teacher has instructed.
7. The teacher listens in on students talk and reteaches as needed.
8. Ask several students to share their thinking.
9. The teacher guides the students practicing the strategy at several stopping points.

Small Group (Strategy Lessons)

Strategy Lessons work well for reteaching students with similar needs. Strategy lessons include students of multiple reading levels, who require reteaching of the same strategy. The teacher models the strategy for instruction and students practice using a familiar text at their instructional or independent reading level.

Procedures for Independent Reading

Students read independently at their independent reading level. In the primary grades many times this is a rereading of guided reading books, shared reading texts, poems, songs, nursery rhymes or new easy texts. Students read at their independent reading level with a partner, during centers, or during teacher selected reading times.

During Independent Reading

- Students need to read at an independent reading level which where they can read 95-100% of the words correctly. Independent reading should be done at school and at home for at least one - two hours a week. This allows students to practice on fluency and comprehension.

- For some of the reading time, students should be allowed to select texts about topics that they enjoy. This promotes a love and enjoyment of reading.

- Students need to understand when they are reading at the correct level. Try using the bicycle example: Riding up the hill – hard text, riding down the hill – easy text, riding on level ground – just right text.

- Model and provide many opportunities for rereading. Rereading is a very important skill that many students feel is unnecessary. Rereading is like watching a movie you love over and over again. It can offer many opportunities for students to think about the parts they love, the parts they don't understand, and notice new elements.

- During independent reading students discuss their thoughts and questions with a teacher, a partner or with classmates in a small group.

- During independent reading students can jot down ideas, questions, and responses on a sticky note or in a student response journal. Remind students to include page numbers on their sticky notes and student response journals to help them locate the pages where they want to talk. This holds their thinking until time to discuss with a partner, or in a small group.

- Students use boxes, bags or baskets to organize and hold their independent reading texts. This allows students to quickly access books for daily independent and partnership reading.

Partnerships

Partnerships are set up with similar reading levels (from the guided reading groups) or varied levels. Example: Teachers observe students during guided reading and pair students who can work well together. When pairing students with varied levels the teacher with four different levels of reading groups labeled A-D would group A with C, and B with D.

Partnership Reading is two students reading either at the same level of reading or mixed level. The teacher observes students to select students that can work well together as partners. AEA has found that partnering students from the Guided Reading Group or like levels work best. These students have many of the same texts and can read new texts at the same reading level which provides many opportunities to work together. Partners can read together taking turns reading and then discussing or they can read independently and get together later to discuss. These partners stay together as long as the students are growing as readers. Teachers occasionally sit in on partnerships to monitor the students as they work with partners. As the teacher monitors partnerships at work she makes notes about future mini-lessons or strategy lessons. The teachers role is to also make sure students are reading texts that are on their independent reading level. The teacher evaluates students' progress through conferences, records of student observation, reading response journals, etc.

AEA has provided a Discussion Wheel for K-2 to use during independent partnership reading that allows the teacher to angle student's talk during partnership reading. Introduce, model and practice using the Discussion Wheel before releasing the students to use the chart independently in partnership reading.

The wheel is divided into four sections, each containing a strategy icon and key phrase to be used to angle students talk during partnership reading. The wheel works as a tool for the teacher to prompt students to practice a specific strategy that has been introduced during partnership reading. The teacher indicates the strategy for practice by placing a paper clip, or close pin on icon for the strategy. The wheel can be placed in students book bags or book boxes before students arrive at school to promote independence. Students arrive at school and go immediately to their partnership reading area and select a book from their book bag or book box and start their partnership reading and discussion. This is an introduction for primary students to read, think and discuss texts using the strategies introduced.

Options:

- Partnership developed in Small Group Reading provides a partner to discuss strategies during "stop to talk".

- AEA uses Partnership Reading at the end of the Small Group Reading Lesson allowing students to continue to read and practice after the lesson.

- As students begin to read longer texts the students practice strategies with the teacher in a Guided Reading Lesson using stopping points. Students can continue reading with a partner after the Guided Reading Lesson has ended to continue practicing the strategy.

- Students may also work with a partner after small group reading to complete graphic organizers, discuss the texts, complete activities related to the strategy taught during the small group lesson.

- AEA recommends that students be given many opportunities to read with partners each day. This could include arrival to class, during centers, after guided reading lesson, after lunch, or before going home, etc. Students use baskets, magazine boxes or bags to hold their independent reading texts, providing organization and a quick transition to meet with a partner to reread and discuss books.

- AEA has provided a Reading With a Partner Chart for K-2 to provide a step by step guide for students during partnership reading. Introduce, model and practice the steps and how to use the Reading With a Partner Chart before releasing the students to use the chart independently in partnership reading. Post the chart where it is visible for students during partnership reading or provide a small chart in book bags or book boxes.

Procedural Mini-Lessons

Procedural Mini-lessons
Introduction

- During the first few weeks of school, it is imperative to teach students all the basic workings of the classroom. Everything from where to sit, how to transition, ways to respond, etc., must be taught explicitly and practiced repeatedly to ensure that students know what to do during every minute of their instructional day. All other teaching will lose effectiveness if classroom management has not been addressed first.

- Procedural mini-lessons, like all other mini-lessons, should be taught by defining what students need to do and why they are learning to do it. Each of the following mini-lessons needs to be taught and revisited until the students have all routines and procedures well-established.

Note: It is important to note that procedural mini-lessons will need to be adjusted according to the grade and developmental level of the students being taught. Definitions and procedures can be modified and adjusted to meet the varying needs of each grade level and classroom set-up.

Getting Ready to Read
A Place to Read (Week 1 and 2)

Materials: Chart of A Place to Read

- Prepare and display the A Place to Read Definition Chart shown below. A blackline master is also provided on the PDR-CD. The teacher should enlarge the chart, create their own example of the chart or make a transparency to show the students.

- Use the definition chart to introduce the procedural mini-lesson.

A Place to Read

Readers need a quiet place to read and think.

- Quiet reading time—voices off
- Conferencing—2-inch voice
- Partner Reading or Station Work—indoor voice

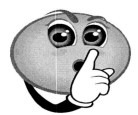

- ***We need a quiet place to read so that our thinking is not disturbed and we can understand what we are reading.***
- Appropriate noise level will vary from activity to activity. It is important to teach and reteach, through modeling, and practicing the appropriate noise level for each activity.

- Teachers can monitor noise level by using signal devices such as stop lights (red—too noisy, yellow—be careful, green—we are working) as visual signals to the students that they are working at the appropriate noise level.

- Teachers may want to include some other optional noise levels signal devices such as hand signals, soft bells, or dimmed lighting to warn students about their noise level.

Working in Stations

Materials: Chart of Work Stations

- Prepare and display the Work Stations Definition Chart shown below. A blackline master is also provided on the PDR-CD. The teacher should enlarge the chart, create their own example of the chart or make a transparency to show the students.

- Use the definition chart to introduce procedural mini-lesson.

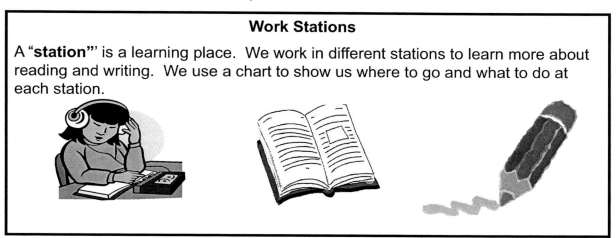

Work Stations

A "**station**"' is a learning place. We work in different stations to learn more about reading and writing. We use a chart to show us where to go and what to do at each station.

- Introduce, model and practice the following procedures using a chart of stations used in your classroom.
    - How to read/find your name/activity on the stations chart
    - How to appropriately compete the activity at each station
    - How to move quickly and quietly from station to station

- Station charts will vary from classroom to classroom. Most station charts have student/group names (or photographs) to represent the students and activity cards that pictorially represent each station (i.e. a picture of a book for the independent reading station) that can be moved around and changed out as stations are added or deleted.

- It is better to start with one activity/station (such as independent reading) and teach/practice that station until the students can perform that activity very well before adding another station to the chart.

- The key to effectively using stations is organization and consistent training on the part of the teacher and effectively following directions on the part of the students.

Falling in Love with Reading

Talking About Your Reading

Materials: Chart of Talking About Your Reading

- Prepare and display the Talking About Your Reading Chart shown below. A blackline master is also provided on the PDR-CD. The teacher should enlarge the chart, create their own example of the chart or make a transparency to show the students.

Talking About Reading

The more good books we read, the more we love reading. Sharing our favorite books helps everyone know how much we love reading.

- Use the chart to introduce the procedural mini-lesson.

  - Bring a favorite book or books to share with the students. Use your book(s) to share and discuss the following :

    - Talking about your favorite book
    - Sharing your favorite part and tell why
    - Discussing who reads to you at home
    - Describing your favorite place to read
    - Telling what you like best about reading

    - Ask students to bring one of their favorite books to school and use the questions above to share and discuss their books.

Where and How to Sit During Reading Time

Materials: Chart of Where and How to Sit During Reading Time

- Prepare and display the We Love Reading Chart shown below. A blackline master is also provided on the PDR-CD.

Where and How to Sit During Reading

During reading time, we **sit** and **listen** to the teacher read.

- Teachers should enlarge the chart, create their own example of the chart or make a transparency to show the students.

- Use the chart to introduce procedural mini-lesson.

- ***During reading time, we sit and listen to the teacher read. Knowing where and how to sit will help us move quickly and quietly to the carpet so we are ready to learn.***

- Introduce, model and practice the following procedures:
  - Coming quickly and quietly come to the carpet
  - Knowing where and how to sit during reading time (criss-cross, sit up straight, eyes ahead, hands in lap, ready to learn)
  - Moving quickly and quietly from the carpet back to desks/tables
  - Talking about why is it important

"Tuning In" During Read Aloud

Materials: Chart of "Tuning In" During Read Aloud

- Prepare and display the "Tuning In" during reading aloud chart shown below. A blackline master is also provided on the PDR-CD. The teacher should enlarge the chart, create their own example of the chart or make a transparency to show the students.

- Use the chart to introduce procedural mini-lesson.

"Tune In" During Read Aloud

We listen to the story with our eyes, ears, and an alert mind.

Look	Listen	Alert Mind

During reading time, we listen to the story with our eyes, ears, and mind awake so that we can understand and enjoy the stories we hear.

- Teach and Discuss:
  - What does 'good listening' look like?
  - What does it mean to have eyes, ears and mind awake?
  - How to "tune in during read aloud"
  - Listen with eyes, ears, and mind
  - How will listening with an awake mind help us understand and enjoy the story?

Working as a Community

Materials: Chart of Working as a Community

- Prepare and display the Working as a Community Chart shown below. A blackline master is also provided on the PDR-CD. The teacher should enlarge the chart, create their own example of the chart or make a transparency to show the students.

- Use the chart to introduce procedural mini-lesson.

Working as a Community

A community of learners is like a **"school family"** that always helps one another learn.

- *When we work well together, we become a community of learners. A community of learners is like a "school family" that always helps one another learn.*
- Introduce, model and practice the following concepts.
  - What is a "family"?
  - What is a "school family"?
  - How do family members help each other?
  - Teach mutual respect/cooperation
  - How can we become a "community of learners"?

Reading with a Partner

Materials: Chart of Reading with a Partner

- Prepare and display the Reading with a Partner Chart shown below. A blackline master is also provided on the PDR-CD. The teacher should enlarge the chart; create their own example of the chart of make a transparency to show the students.

- Use the definition chart to introduce procedural mini-lesson.

Partner Reading

- **Read the title.**
- **Look at the pictures.**
- **Make a prediction.**
- **Read to your partner.**
- **Tell your favorite part.**

- *We read with partners to practice our reading and share our thoughts about the books we read. This helps us all become better readers.*

Introduce, model and practice the following procedures:

- Finding your partner's name (see station chart)
- Selecting books (partner browsing bags with multiple copies of the same text)
- Deciding how/where to sit—(quickly and quietly, criss-cross, sit up straight, books in lap, ready to learn)
- Taking turns (read a page while partner follows/stop to share; switch roles)
- Using appropriate voice level (quiet "conversation" voices)

How to Share - With a Partner

Materials: Chart of How to Choose a Book

- Prepare and display the How to Share – With a Partner Chart shown below. A blackline master is also provided on the PDR-CD. The teacher should enlarge the chart, create their own example of the chart or make a transparency to show the students.

How to Share – With a Partner

1. Turn to your partner.
2. Speak

- Use the chart to introduce the procedural mini-lesson.

- ***When we turn and talk to a partner, we are 'sharing'. When we share, we need to speak and listen carefully. When we listen and speak respectfully, we learn more about ourselves, our partners, and the books we read.***

Introduce, model and practice the following procedures:

- Turning and talking to a partner
- Sitting "knee-to-knee"
- Looking at your partner when he/she is speaking
- Listening carefully
- Waiting for your turn to share
- Speaking clearly
- Talking about your book (or the objective being taught)
- Treating your partner with respect

How to Share—With a Whole Group

Materials: Chart of How to Choose a Book

- Prepare and display the Reading with a Partner Chart shown below. A blackline master is also provided on the PDR-CD. The teacher should enlarge the chart; create their own example of the chart of make a transparency to show the students.

How to Share – With a Whole Group

1. Sit or Stand
2. Talk Clearly

- Use the definition chart to introduce procedural mini-lesson.

- ***When a student sits/stands in front of a group and talks about their reading, they are 'sharing'. When a student shares, the audience needs to listen respectfully so that everyone learns from each other.***

Introduce, model and practice the following procedures:

- Listening as an audience
- Looking at the speaker when he/she is sharing
- Speaking clearly (head up)
- Listening carefully
- Asking appropriate questions at the appropriate time

Using Books to Grow as a Reader (Week 3 and 4)

How to Take Care of Books

Materials: Chart of How to Take Care of Books

- Make a chart of How to Take Care of Books to use when introducing the procedure. (Prepare chart before or during lesson.)
- ***We have great books to read in our classroom library. Learning the right way to take care of books will help our books last a long time so that everyone can enjoy them.***

Introduce, model and practice the following procedures:

- Opening and holding books (both hands, clean fingers, don't bend/break the spine)
- Turning pages (top down)
- Keeping your place (use bookmarks – no "dog-ears")
- Marking your place and closing books down (closed with bookmark)
- Showing respect (be careful not to draw in books or tear pages)
- Checking out books (procedures)

How to Choose a Book

Materials: Chart of How to Choose a Book

- Make a chart of How to Choose a Book and use to introduce the procedure.
- ***Choosing the right book is very important. If a book is too easy, we will not learn as much. If a book is too hard, we won't understand what we are reading. If we choose a 'just right' book, we will learn how to be a better reader.***

Introduce, model and practice the following procedures:

- Knowing if a book is 'too hard' (struggles through words; can't remember or understand what was read)
- Knowing if a book is 'too easy' (no new/unknown words; familiar/memorized text)
- Knowing if a book is 'just right' (can use "Goldilocks and the Three Bears" analogy)
- Using the five finger rule: If you read a page and have five or more mistakes, the book is too hard.

Keeping a Reading Log

Materials: Chart of Keeping a Reading Log

- Make a chart of How to Keep a Reading Log and use to introduce the procedure.
- ***Students keep track of their reading in a log. This helps the student and teacher see and remember all the different kinds of books the student has read.***

Introduce, model and practice the following procedures:
- Using a reading log (record author, title, etc.)
- Maintaining the reading log and sharing with others

Where to Keep Books for Independent Reading

Materials: Chart of Where to Keep Books for Independent Reading

- Make a chart of Where to Keep Books for Independent Reading and use to introduce the procedure.
- ***Students have 'just right' books they can read by themselves or with a partner. These independent reading books need to be kept in their 'home' until it is time to read them. When we are finished reading, we need to return books to their proper place so that we will always know where to find them.***

Introduce, model and practice the following procedures:
- Selecting independent reading books
- Check out and returning books to their "home"
- Storing independent reading books: browsing bags, baskets/tubs, pocket charts, cubbies, etc.
- Returning and selecting independent reading books
- Discussing why this is this important

Reading with a Partner

Materials: Chart of Reading with a Partner

- Make a chart How to Read With a Partner to use to introduce the procedure.
- Students read with partners to share stories and learn from each other. When students read with a partner, they need to work together in a respectful way.

Introduce, model and practice the following procedures:
- Knowing where and how to sit
- Taking turns
- Listening with a an alert mind
- Showing respect during partner discusssion

Drawing and Writing Responses about Reading

Materials: Chart of Drawing and Writing Responses about Reading

- Make a chart of How to Draw and Write Responses to Reading and use to introduce the procedure.
- Students write or draw about the books they read to help them think more deeply about their reading.

Introduce, model and practice the following procedures:
- Thinking Deeply when drawing and writing responses to reading
- Using the correct format when drawing or writing a response to reading
  - Date
  - Author and title
  - Personal response or connection
- Drawing a picture in the appropriate place on the page
  - Placement on page

Key Cognitive Strategies

What are Cognitive Strategies?
How do they Improve Comprehension?

For many years, researchers have been working to understand how proficient readers create meaning and reading comprehension during the reading process. In 1968 E.B. Huey, in <u>Learning to Read at School, the Early Period (p342)</u> wrote that children must "come to think of reading as the getting or giving of thought from what is written, rather than as a naming of certain written words".

For the past 30 years researchers have been studying proficient readers and examining what happens 'in their heads', in order to discover ways of improving reading comprehension instruction.

Predicting, questioning, visualizing, retelling, summarizing, defining, connecting, and rereading are the strategies that current research has proven to be most effective in fostering students' progress and growth as active readers. AEA recommends that these strategies be taught early in comprehension instruction for primary readers because they will coach students to become active listeners and readers. PDR has included a definition, key phrases and an icon for each of these strategies. These strategies should be introduced, modeled, practiced and quickly integrated into daily reading as other strategies are being taught.

> *Keys to Unlock Meaning*
> *"In the 1980's, a breakthrough occurred: Researchers identified the specific thinking strategies used by proficient readers. They found that reading is an interactive process in which good readers engage in a constant internal dialogue with the text. The ongoing dialogue helps them understand and elaborate on what they read. By identifying what good readers do as they read, this research gave important new insights about how to teach children to read it and get it."*
>
> *Zimmermann, Susan and Chryse Hutchins. 7 Keys to Comprehension: How to Help Your Kids Read It and Get It!*
> Crown Publishing Group., 2003

Additional information and teacher plans for these cognitive strategies can be found in the **STOP TO THINK** Program.

Predict

What: (What is prediction?) Readers take information from the text and what they know to make a smart guess about what might happen in the future and set a purpose for reading. Readers provide evidence for their thinking by sharing information from the text that led them to make their predictions.

Why: (Why does it help you as a reader?) Making predictions helps the reader remain engaged throughout the reading and will confirm their understanding of the text.

When: (When is it used during reading?) Predictions are used before reading to encourage students to use their prior knowledge to predict what might happen in the story. During reading students confirm, change or make new predictions. After reading readers revisit their predictions in order to understand why their thinking was correct or incorrect.

How: (How does a good reader predict when they read?) Think aloud to model prediction. Additional information can be found in the STOP TO THINK Guide and in the Inference section of Developing Readers Primary.

Predict

Predict or "make a guess" about what will happen. Tell why you made that prediction.

Key Phrase:
- I predict _____ because _____.
- My prediction was right because _____.
- I am changing my prediction because_____.

Expectations

Predict			
Grade Introduced - I **Grade Developed - D**	K	1	2
Reading	I	D	D
Writing			

Connect

Teacher Talk

What: (What is connect?)
Readers use their personal experiences to make connections to characters, events, feelings, and locations.

Why: (Why does it help you as a reader?) Making connections with the text helps readers relate, understand, revise their thinking and remember the text.

When: (When is it used during reading?) Good readers compare their personal experiences with the text before, during, and after reading.

How: (How does a good reader make connections when they read?) Think aloud to model connections. Additional information can be found in the <u>STOP TO THINK</u> Guide.

Connect

When reading make connections to books and ...
- what you know.
- other books you have read.
- things going on in the world.

Key Phrase:

- This reminds me of_____.

- I remember when _____.
- I connect to _____.

Expectations

Strategy Name: Connect			
Grade Introduced – I **Grade Developed - D**	K	1	2
Reading	I	D	D
Writing		I	D

Describe

Teacher Talk

What: (What is describe the picture in your mind?) Active readers use their senses and emotions to create mental pictures or movies in their minds as they read. Their understanding of vocabulary terms and knowledge of the world helps them create their mental picture.

Why: (Why does it help you as a reader?) Creating a picture helps the reader organize the text, making a time-line in their head of the events. Visualizing the text helps them remember the text.

When: (When is it used during reading?) Readers create mental pictures when listening to or reading a text using what they know about the events, setting, characters and facts in the text.

How: (How does a good reader make a mental picture in their mind?) Think aloud to model how a good reader describes the mental picture in their head. Additional information can be found in the <u>STOP TO THINK</u> Guide.

Describe

Make a mental movie in your mind as you read. Describe the picture you see in your head.

Key Phrase:
- The picture I see in my mind is _____.
- I see _____.

Expectations

Describe			
Grade Introduced – I **Grade Developed - D**	K	1	2
Reading	I	D	D
Writing			

Ask a Question

Teacher Talk

What: (What is questioning?) Good readers wonder and question characters, events and situations in the text. They use prior knowledge to question when, where, what will happen and why.

Why: (Why does it help you as a reader?) Asking questions helps readers remain engaged as they search for answers. This also clarifies and monitors a reader's understanding of the text.

When: (When is it used during reading?) Good readers ask questions before, during and after reading. They ask questions using their prior knowledge to confirm ideas or look to the text to provide new knowledge.

How: (How does a good reader ask questions during reading?) Think aloud to model how a good reader asks questions when reading. Additional information can be found in the STOP TO THINK Guide.

Ask a Question

Readers ask questions or wonder about characters, events, and situations in the story. They talk about what made them wonder.

Key Phrases
- I'm wondering_____ because_____.
- Why is _____ happening?

Expectations

Ask a Question			
Grade Introduced – I **Grade Developed - D**	K	1	2
Reading	I	D	D
Writing **K-Dictate, 1st - Independent**	I	I	D

Reread

Teacher Talk

What: (What is rereading?) Good readers monitor their reading and reread when they have lost focus or understanding. Proficient readers use rereading to clarify the text and understand the author's messages.

Why: (Why does it help you as a reader?) Rereading helps readers clarify meaning, look for new information, create or correct the mental picture and stay connected.

When: (When is it used during reading?) Rereading is used during and after reading to clarify the author's message. Readers reread a text many times to look for information, to revisit their favorite parts, to review parts they don't understand, to reread for fluency, or to recreate a time-line in their head of events that happened in the story.

How: (How does a good reader reread during reading?) Think aloud to model how a good reader rereads during reading. Additional information can be found in the STOP TO THINK Guide.

Reread

Good readers reread to make sure they understand.

Key Phrases
- **That didn't sound right. I need to reread.**
- **That didn't look like right. I need to reread.**
- **That didn't make sense. I need to reread.**
- **I like this part. I want to reread.**

Expectations

Reread			
Grade Introduced – I **Grade Developed - D**	**K**	**1**	**2**
Reading	I	D	D
Writing			

Define

Teacher Talk

What: (What is define?) Readers use information in the text, word study and what they know to define and clarify words and phrases in the text. Defining words and phrases in the text requires readers to monitor their comprehension.

Why: (Why does it help you as a reader?) Defining new words and clarifying the text helps the reader get a clearer picture of what the author is trying to say.

When: (When is it used during reading?) During reading readers use prior knowledge, context clues or dictionaries to define unknown words or terms in the text and words with multiple meanings.

How: (How does a good reader define new words during reading?) Think aloud to model how a good reader searches and readers during reading to locate context clues to help define new words. Additional information can be found in the <u>STOP TO THINK</u> Guide.

Define

Define new words in the text by using clues in the text and what you already know.

Key Phrases
- I know this means_____ because _____.
- I think I understand _____because the author tells me_____?
- I can read _____because I know the word part _____.

Expectations

Define			
Grade Introduced – I **Grade Developed - D**	K	1	2
Reading	I	D	D
Writing			

Retell

Teacher Talk

What: (What is retell?) Readers must be able to organize the events in the story and distinguish between details and important parts.

Why: (Why does it help you as a reader?) Retelling helps readers because they must remember the text and organize it in their minds to create a time line of events.

When: (When is it used during reading?) During and after reading readers use their mental timeline to retell the important events.

How: (How does a good reader rereads during reading?) Think aloud to model how a good reader retells events during reading. Additional information can be found in the STOP TO THINK Guide.

Retell

Retell the story telling the important parts in the order as they happened.

Key Phrases

- The first thing that happened was _____.
- Next, _____
- Then _____ happened.
- Finally, _____.

Expectations

Retell			
Grade Introduced - I **Grade Developed - D**	K	1	2
Reading	I	D	D
Writing			

Summary

Teacher Talk

What: (What is summarize?) Summarizing the text requires the reader to pick out the most important ideas to retell the story in a few sentences.

Why: (Why does it help you as a reader?) Summarizing what the text is mostly about helps the reader understand the author's message by keeping the reader focused on the main idea.

When: (When is it used during reading?) Summarizing the text is done at the conclusion of the text.

How: (How does a good reader rereads during reading?) Think aloud to model how a good reader summarizes after reading. Additional information can be found in the STOP TO THINK Guide and the Summary section in Developing Readers Primary.

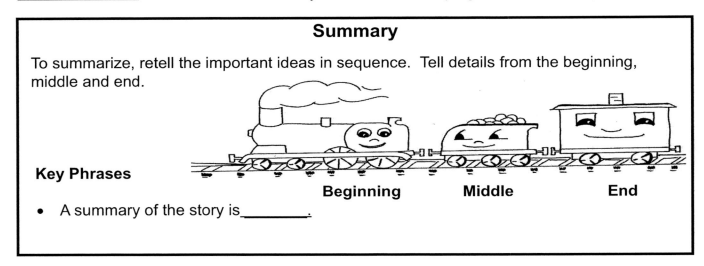

Summary

To summarize, retell the important ideas in sequence. Tell details from the beginning, middle and end.

Key Phrases

- A summary of the story is_____.

Beginning   Middle   End

Expectations

Summary			
Grade Introduced – I **Grade Developed - D**	K	1	2
Reading	I	D	D
Writing			I

Vocabulary

Context Clues

Context Clues

Teacher Talk

What: (What is a context clue?): Sometimes when reading or listening to a text, an unknown word is seen or heard. Readers listen or look for clues in the text to determine the word's meaning. The words and sentences around the unknown word can give the reader clues. These clues are called context clues. Sometimes they are found close to the new word. Sometimes the reader must listen or look in the paragraph before or after the word. The reader also must use information provided in the text and what makes sense to figure out the meaning of the word.

Why: (Why does it help you as a reader?): The reader must understand the unknown word before he can understand what the author is saying.

When: (When do you use it during reading?) This strategy is used when the reader comes to an unknown word and there are suitable context clues within the text to figure out the meaning.

What does research tell us about this strategy?
Eileen Carr and Karen Wixsom (1986) provide four guidelines for evaluating vocabulary instruction. Students should: relate new vocabulary to background knowledge, develop elaborated word knowledge, be actively involved in learning, and develop strategies for acquiring vocabulary independently.
Carr E.& Wixsom, K.K. (1986). Guidelines for evaluating vocabulary instruction. *Journal of Reading, 29*. p. 588-595.

What is expected at this level when using the strategy?
Younger students will learn to decipher word connotations through meaningful experiences. They must be given explicit opportunities to attach meaning to words from concrete experiences. Older students can develop vocabulary through listening to and reading text. They can use both experiences and context in print to decipher meaning.

What prior knowledge or schema do the students need to have?
The context clues should be familiar to the children.

What are the cautions and tips when teaching this strategy?
- When selecting a text for small group instruction, plan for both the struggling and the advanced reader.
- If the text is too hard for the students, then they will not be able to read clues about the unknown word. They will all be unknown words.
- If the text is too easy for the students, then they may not come to an unknown word.
- In working to introduce and develop skill, initially chose texts that provide clear contextual clues that are in close proximity to the target word

- Students at this age that are reading above level may not have the experience of using context clues. Even if a child is an accurate word caller, they may not know the meaning of every word they encounter. They are unaware of when they come to an unknown word because they are not stopping to think about the text. This is often why a wonderful word caller has trouble with comprehension.
- Some students will know the unknown word that was chosen. They may need to be reminded to let others find the meaning of the unknown word on their own.
- When reading in the content areas, the students may not have the prior experiences to make connections with the unknown word. Therefore, the teacher will need to help develop that knowledge (build schema) with/for the students.

Expectations

Context Clues			
Grade Introduced- I Grade Developed- D	K	1	2
Reading	I	D	D
Writing			

Context Clues

Introduction

Materials: Context Clues Definition Chart

- Prepare and display the Context Clues Definition Chart shown below. A blackline master is also provided on the PDR-CD. The teacher should enlarge the chart, create their own example of the chart, or make a transparency to show the students.

- Use the definition chart to introduce the strategy. Name and define the strategy, including why and when to use the strategy during reading. (Refer to Teacher Talk)

- When discussing the definition and key phrases use an example of a situation or familiar book to activate prior knowledge about the strategy prediction.

Context Clues

When you read a story there may be words you don't know. Look for context clues to help you know the meaning of the new word.

I was pleased, or happy.

Key Phrases
- I think the word _____ means _____ because _____.
- The context clues that helped me know the word are _____.

- Display and discuss the Definition Chart.

Model

Activity 1

Materials: Context Clues Definition Chart
Chart paper

- *Sometimes when I am reading, I come to a word I do not know.*

- *I am going to see if context clues can help me in reading the unknown words.*

- Write the following sentence on the board and read it aloud to the students:

    Dad went fishing and caught a carp at the lake.

- *I want you to think about what you know about the word. What information or "context clues" helped you understand what a marigold is?*

- *Turn to your partner and say: I know _____ about the word marigolds.*

- Ask several students to share what they know about the word marigolds. Students should share garden, beautiful, and gold. Underline these words in the sentence on the board.

- *Looking at these clues, who would like to share what they think a marigold is?*

- After the students have responded, ask, *How did you come to that decision?*

What did you use? How did you know?

- After reading ask students to talk to their partner the new words they found during reading and the clues in the text that helped them know the meaning.

Option: Ask students to use their response journal to write down new words. Write the word and the clues that helped them know the new word.

Guided Practice

    Materials: Context Clues Definition Chart
                 Text with 4-5 words with context clues to use for modeling
                 Sticky notes

- Review the Context Clues Definition Chart with the students.

- Preread the text and locate 3-5 words with context clues to model during think aloud. Using sticky notes write down what you will model during think aloud starting with key phrases. Place sticky notes on the pages where you will stop to model.

- *In the last few days we have been learning how we can use clues to know the meaning of new words. Today as I read _____ I will stop and show you how I find clues in the text to know what the meaning of the word.*

- After modeling how to locate context clues 3-4 times in the text ask students to give it a try. Continue to read and stop at the last selected word with context clues.

- *This time I want you to give it a try. Turn to your partner and say, I know the word _____ means _____. The clues that helped me know the new word are _____.*

- Allow students enough time to share their thinking with their partner. Ask several students to share their thinking and discuss.

Shared Reading

> Materials: Text with 3-5 words with context clues
> Sticky notes

- Preread the text and locate 3-5 words with context clues to practice during the shared reading. Use sticky notes to mark stopping points. Write the key phrases on your sticky notes to start the student talk. Example: Turn to your partner and say: The context clues that helped me know the word _____ are _____. Students turn and talk to their partner and discuss the context clues that helped them know the word.

- ***We have been practicing using context clues to help us find the meaning of unknown words. Today as we read our story, you will hear words that are unfamiliar to you.***

- ***As we read I will stop when I come to new words. I will ask you to turn to your partner and say, The clues that helped me know the meaning of the words are _____.***

- Allow students enough time to share their thinking with their partner. Ask several students to share their thinking and discuss.

Note: If needed reread the sentence and help them find the meaning of the word using context clues. Stress the importance of understanding the meanings of words as they try to understand what they are hearing.

Small Group Reading

> Material: Texts read during small group

- As books are introduced to students on their instructional reading level, ask students to mark one or two unknown words with a sticky note as they read.

- After reading, make a chart of the unknown words they encountered. Have the students use context clues to find the meaning of the unknown words. Keep the chart in sight so the students can see new words being added to their vocabulary.

Read Aloud – Multiple Strategies Practice

> Materials: New Picture books for Read Aloud
> 3-4 Introduced strategies for practice

- As new strategies are introduced it is important to continue to practice previously introduced strategies and orchestrate them with the new strategy. Select 3-4 strategies that have been introduced in previous lessons to review and practice with the new strategy.

- Set up the read aloud by selecting appropriate places to stop in the text to practice the strategies selected. Prepare a sticky note for each strategy writing a key phrase for the strategy to be practiced. The sticky notes are placed on the page as a signal as you read to stop and ask the students to turn to their partner and practice the strategy. Example: ***Turn to your partner and say, I predict _____. Tell you partner what you predict and why.***

- Allow students enough time to share their thinking with their partner. Ask several students to share their thinking and discuss.

- Continue to read until you come to the next stopping point. Repeat practicing another selected strategy.

Note: Select texts that support the strategies for practice. Example strategies practiced could be; predicting, asking a question, describe a character, setting, and summary.

Independent Practice

  Materials: Texts on independent reading levels

- Students select and read a text on their independent reading level. As they come to a word they do not know, have them write it on the context clues graphic organizer. Beside the word, have the students write the definition and the clue words that helped them understand the meaning.

A Step Beyond

- As students are reading in the content areas, have them keep a list of the unknown words they encounter. They may make a dictionary to keep in which they write the word and its meaning. You can use address books for this. The alphabet is there for the students to guide them in finding the place to write their new word. They are making a book of the new vocabulary they have learned.

- When students share their writing with the class or a small group, invite the listeners to comment on new words they hear and to discuss the context clues the student authors use.

Context Clues
Across the Curriculum

Math	• Students will use context clues when reading story problems. Story problems usually contain key words that provide clues to which mathematical process should be used.
Science	• Students often encounter unknown words in science texts. The use of context clues can help the student determine the meaning of an unknown word.
Social Studies	• Students often encounter unknown words in social studies texts. The use of context clues can help the student determine the meaning of an unknown word.
Other	• Students will use context clues during listening and reading in everyday routines.
Writing	• Students will use meaningful words and phrases in their writing and explain the context clues they have given the reader to help them define meaning.

Synonyms
Antonyms

Synonyms and Antonyms

Teacher Talk

What: (What is an antonym or a synonym?) Synonyms are words that have the same or almost the same meanings, but may influence you in different ways. Example: giggle – laugh, angry – mad. Antonyms are words that have opposite meanings. Example: absent – present, laugh – cry.

Why: (Why does it help you as a reader?) This strategy helps the reader make visual images and better understand the text. The use of these special words can be transferred into writing.

When: (When is it used during reading?) This strategy is used when a visual image of what is being heard or read is desired.

What does research tell us about this strategy?
Eileen Carr and Karen Wixsom (1986) provide four guidelines for evaluating vocabulary instruction. Students should: relate new vocabulary to background knowledge, develop elaborated word knowledge, be actively involved in learning, and develop strategies for acquiring vocabulary independently.
Carr E.& Wixsom, K.K. (1986). Guidelines for Evaluating Vocabulary Instruction. *Journal of Reading, 29*. p.p. 588-595.

What is expected at this level when using the strategy?
Students will use synonyms and antonyms in their listening, speaking, reading, and writing.

What prior knowledge or schema do the students need to have?
Students first develop a knowledge and understanding of synonyms and antonyms in their listening and speaking vocabularies. They need to have an understanding of the concept of things that are alike and things that are different.

What are the cautions and tips when teaching this strategy?

• Antonyms seem to be easier for students at this age than synonyms. You may choose to teach several lessons on antonyms before beginning synonyms.

• Students sometimes confuse the two terms. A simple trick to share is that synonyms are words that mean the same thing. Synonym and same both begin with the letter "s". Antonyms are "against" each other and against begins with "a".

Synonym = **s**ame   **A**ntonyms = **a**gainst

• Encourage the students to use synonyms in their writing. You may write some of the most frequently used words on large sheets of paper. Have the students work together to brainstorm synonyms for each word. Hang the "mini-posters" up in the room. As they are using one of the frequent words in their writing, encourage them to check out the poster for "word choice" for a synonym they could use instead.

Example:	big	large
	giant	huge
	enormous	etc.

• As the students encounter other synonyms for the words in their reading, they add to the poster.

• Students need to have a word in their listening, speaking vocabulary before they can use it to find synonyms and antonyms in their reading and writing.

Expectations

Synonyms and Antonyms			
Grade Introduced – I Grade Developed – D	K	1	2
Reading		I	D
Writing			

Synonyms and Antonyms

Introduction

Materials: Synonyms and Antonyms Definition Chart

- Prepare and display the Synonyms and Antonyms Definition Chart shown below. A blackline master is also provided on the PDR-CD. The teacher should enlarge the chart, create their own example of the chart, or make a transparency to show the students.

- Use the definition chart to introduce the strategy. Name and define the strategy, including why and when to use the strategy during reading. (Refer to Teacher Talk)

Antonyms are words that mean the opposite.

Examples: hot   cold

Synonyms are words that mean the same thing.

Examples: big   large

Key Phrases:
- I think _____ means the same as _____.
- I think _____ means the opposite as _____.

- Display and review the Synonyms and Antonyms Definition Chart.
- When discussing the definition and key phrases use an example of a situation or familiar book to activate prior knowledge about the strategy prediction.

Model – Antonyms

Materials: Synonyms and Antonyms Definitions Chart

- ***Sometimes when I am reading, it helps me to know the antonyms of words. Antonyms can change the meaning of the text.***

- Write these sentences on the board or chart and read them aloud:

    I have a **big** ball.   I have a **small** ball.

- ***In these two sentences, big and small are antonyms. They are opposites.***

They mean completely different things. Switching the word "big" with its opposite "small" changes the meaning of the text.

- *I can see why it is important for me to understand antonyms.*
- Use the examples below or select additional words to use for practice. Say the word and think aloud of a word that is the opposite and write it on the board or chart.

    little – big   fast – slow   up – down   happy – sad

- *Now, I want you to give it a try. Let's see if you can find an antonym for these words.* Use the words below and ask the students to turn and talk about an antonym for the word.
- *Turn to your partner and say: _____ means the opposite of_____.*

    go – stop   top – bottom   high – low   soft - hard

- Allow students enough time to share their thinking with their partner. Ask several students to share their thinking and discuss. This will allow them to see that words have more than one word that means the opposite.

Option: Make a chart of these words for students to use in writing. Continue to add to this chart during reading and writing providing students with a chart of antonyms to use in other activities.

Model – Synonyms

> Materials: Synonyms and Antonyms Definitions Chart

- Display and review the Synonyms and Antonyms Definition Chart. Think aloud and explain the definition to the students. Use pictures from familiar books to illustrate the definition.
- *We have talked about antonyms and how they are words that have opposite meanings. Today I am going to think about synonyms. Our definition says that synonyms are words that mean the same or almost the same.*
- *Just as knowing antonyms helps me be a better reader, I think knowing synonyms will also help me be a better reader.*
- Write these sentences on the board and read them aloud:

    Joe **laughed** as he watched the movie.

    Joe **giggled** as he watched the movie.

- *As I read these two sentences, I think the synonyms are laughed and giggled. They mean the same thing. They are something Joe did because he thought the movie was funny.*
- *Authors think about using the synonyms that best fit into their story. I think*

knowing synonyms would help me better understand what the author is telling me.

- *Now, I want you to think about synonyms.*

- Write these words on the board and read each word aloud:

    little   loud   fast   happy

- *Today, I want you to stop to talk and think of synonyms for each of these words. Remember, that synonyms have the same meaning. Turn to your partner and say, A synonym for little is …*

    Example: little, small, tiny, itsy bitsy, etc.

- Allow students enough time to share their thinking with their partner. Ask several students to share their thinking and discuss.

- Repeat this with each word.

Guided Practice
Activity 1

    Materials: Synonyms and Antonyms Definitions Chart

                 Prepare a chart or transparency of <u>A Trip to the Zoo</u>

- Display and review the Synonyms and Antonyms Definition Chart.

- *Today we are going to revise a story using synonyms.*

- Display the chart or transparency of <u>A Trip to the Zoo</u>. A blackline master is provided on the PDR-CD.

- *As we come to one of the underlined words, we will replace it with a synonym of that word. Let's give it a try.*

- Read the story with the students. As you come to an underlined word, have the students share synonyms that could replace the word. Select one of the responses, and write it above the underlined word. Continue this process until you have completed the story.

- *Now let's go back and reread the story with our new words.* Read the story together.

- *We changed some of the words in the story. Did we change the meaning of the story? Why or why not? Turn to your partner and stop to talk and share your thinking.*

- *We did change the words in our story but did not change the meaning of our story. The meaning of the story did not change because we replaced words with synonyms or words that mean the same thing.*

Activity 2

   Materials: Synonyms and Antonyms Definition Chart
   Chart – <u>A Trip to the Zoo</u>

- Follow the same lesson as in Activity 1, and this time replace them with antonyms. The story will take on a completely new meaning. Be sure they understand that the meaning of the story changed because the words were replaced with antonyms, which have opposite meanings.

Activity 3

   Materials: Synonyms and Antonyms Graphic Organizer
   Synonyms and Antonyms Cards

- Cut out the Synonym and Antonym cards that are provided on the PDR-CD.
- Give each student a card and have him/her place it on his/her desk.
- Pass out the graphic organizer. The student will write the word that is on the card on their desk in the appropriate blank. Explain that they are to travel around the classroom and look at the words on their classmates' desks. If the word is an antonym or synonym of their word, they write it in the appropriate space.

Shared Reading

   Materials: Synonyms and Antonyms Definition Chart
   Text for Shared Reading with 3-5 Synonyms for discussion

- Pre-select 3-5 words with synonyms for student discussion.
- During Shared Reading stop at each selected word and ask students to stop to talk to their partners.
- At each stopping point say, ***Turn to your partner and say, a synonym for _____ is _____.***
- Allow students enough time to share their thinking with their partner. Ask several students to share their thinking and discuss. Discuss how this changes the text.

Shared Reading

   Materials: Synonyms and Antonyms Definition Chart
   Text for Shared Reading with 3-5 Antonyms for discussion

- Pre-select 3-5 words with antonyms for student discussion.
- During Shared Reading stop at each selected word and ask students to stop to talk to their partners.
- At each stopping point say, ***Turn to your partner and say, an antonym for _____ is_____.***
- Allow students enough time to share their thinking with their partner. Ask several students to share their thinking and discuss. Discuss how this changes the text

Small Group Reading

Materials: Texts read in small group reading

Student response journals

- After the students have read their books several times, have them choose a page or paragraph from the story. They choose 1-2 words in the selection that they can replace with a synonym.

Options: Revise the story in Shared Writing and replace with a synonym.

Students draw or write the new story using the synonyms for the words they chose in their response journal. Have them share their illustrations or story to the rest of the group.

- Repeat the same activity for antonyms.

Independent Practice

Materials: Texts on independent reading levels

Synonyms and Antonyms Graphic Organizer

- As the students are reading independently, have them select words from the text and complete the Synonyms and Antonyms Graphic Organizer.

- Allow students enough time to share their Synonyms and Antonyms Graphic Organizer with their partner.

- Ask several students to share with the class and discuss.

A Step Beyond

- Prepare a station for the students to play a matching game using antonyms or synonyms. Some students could prepare their own matching game to take home. This game can be played with picture or word cards.

- Some students could use a thesaurus to find a synonym or antonym of a word they are using in their writing.

- Students write a sentence using antonyms and illustrate their sentence.

    Example: Sue hates broccoli, but loves pizza. These could be made into a class book.

- Students can draw or write to create their own book of antonyms and synonyms.

- Younger students can make a T-Chart or fold paper in half and illustrate antonyms.

- Make a chart for "Words to Use" in writing. Record the word, its definition and its synonym or antonym for a reading / writing connection.

Synonyms and Antonyms
Across the Curriculum

Math	• There are some mathematical terms that are synonyms and antonyms: Add / subtract less / fewer More / less more / greater
Science	• Students may use synonyms and antonymswith science terms they encounter: alive / living liquid / solid
Social Studies	• Students may use synonyms and antonyms with social studies terms they encounter: summer / winter
Other	**Music:** loud / soft high / low **Art:** dark / light rough / smooth black / white
Writing "Word Choices"	Make a chart of synonyms and antonyms for students to use during writing.

Base Word

Base Word

Teacher Talk

What: (What is a base word?) A base word is an English word to which prefixes and suffixes are added.

Why: (Why does it help you as a reader?) Students must be able to identify the base word to guide them as they find the meaning of a word in a glossary or dictionary.

When: (When is it used during reading?) Readers use base words, the dictionary, and glossary entries when they come to unknown words.

What does research tell us about this strategy?

"The view of dictionaries that underlies the present research is that a dictionary can provide valuable recourse for language users who reach the limits of their word knowledge. Interaction with a definition, a summary description of a word's meaning, can be an initiating event in learning a word."

McKeown, M.G. (1993). Creating effective definitions for young word learners. *Reading Research Quarterly, 28*(1). P. 16-31.

What is expected at this level when using the strategy?

Students are introduced to and practice using a glossary and beginning dictionary.

What prior knowledge or schema do the students need to have?

Students need to know the alphabet, A B C order, and have the ability to determine and find base words in a dictionary.

What are the cautions and tips when teaching this strategy?

- Students must know their alphabet and alphabetical order before being ready to find the meaning of an unknown word in a glossary or dictionary.

- Students need to be able to alphabetize before using dictionaries. To really use the skill, the dictionary should be on the student's instructional reading level.

- In kindergarten and first grade, students work primarily with base words. Most of these base words will have the inflectional endings 's', 'ed', and 'ing'.

Base word – an English word to which prefixes and suffixes are added.

Root word – a part of a word from a language other than English to which affixes may be added

>　　**Affix** – a word part added to a base word or root word
>
>　　**Prefix** – a letter or letters added to the beginning or the base word.
>　　When a prefix is added, it changes the meaning of the word.
>
>　　**Suffix** – a letter or letters added to the ending of a base word or root word.
>　　When a suffix is added, it changes the meaning of the word.

- Students must know the definition of nouns and verbs (and how to properly identify and use them) before they can compare and contrast them with base words.

Expectations

Base Word			
Grade Introduced – I **Grade Developed - D**	**K**	**1**	**2**
Reading		I	D
Writing			

Base Word

Introduction

Materials: Base Word Definition Chart

- Prepare and display the Base Word Definition Chart shown below. A blackline master is also provided on the PDR-CD. Teachers should enlarge the chart, create their own example of the chart, or make a transparency to show the students.

- Use the definition chart to introduce the strategy. Name and define the strategy, including why and when to use the strategy during reading. (Refer to Teacher Talk)

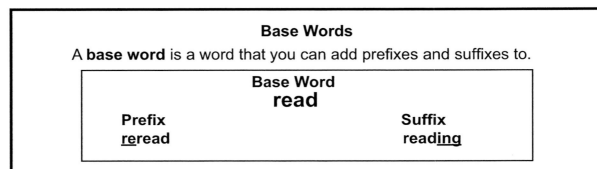

Base Words

A **base word** is a word that you can add prefixes and suffixes to.

Base Word
read

Prefix
<u>re</u>read

Suffix
read<u>ing</u>

- Display and review the Definition Chart.

- When discussing the definition and key phrases use an example of a situation or familiar book to activate prior knowledge about the strategy prediction.

- First graders will be working with base words. Most of the base words they will encounter have the inflectional endings of s, ed, and ing. Root words will be introduced later.

Model

Materials: Base Word Definition Chart

- *Review the Base Word Definition Chart with the students.*

- ***We have been learning how to find the meaning of an unknown word. You can look for context clues to help you figure it out. If context clues don't help, you can use a dictionary to look for the best definition for the unknown word. Sometimes, the unknown word itself is not listed in the dictionary. It has been changed to be used correctly in the sentence. For example, I do not say, John play with his friends. I would say, John plays with his friends.***

- *In order to look up the meaning of the word plays, you must first find the base word, which is play.*

- *Today I am going to practice finding the base word inside of other words. In finding the base word, it is helpful to know what endings are usually added to base words.*

- In first grade, the endings I usually find added to base words are s, ed and ing. When s, ed, and ing are added to the end of a base word, they are called inflectional endings. The letters change the word from singular to plural or change the verb tense. The word remains the same part of speech. If it was a noun, it is still a noun. If it was a verb, it is still a verb.

- *When looking for the base word inside a word, it helps me to think about the word base. A base is used to support or hold something up. The base word 'holds' the other word up. Without the base word, the new word would not exist.*

- *Another way to remember base word is to think of B = Base = Beginning Word*

- *Now I will practice with a few.* Write the following sentence on the board and read it aloud:

      Sally <u>waves</u> to her friends at the beach.

- *I know that there are two kinds of waves. There are waves of water that come to the shore and there is also the wave that people use to greet one another. If I want to look up the word waves in the dictionary, I need to know the base word. I can see the ending that was added was 's'. If I take the 's' away then I have the word wave. Wave is the base word or the word that s was added to.*

- *Now I can look up the word wave and find the best definition for how it was used in my sentence.*

- *I will try a few more:*

  sheds   plays   dogs   helped   sanded   going

- Use think aloud talk as you model finding the base of each word.

- *I think I can now look up words I need to know the meaning of because I know how to find the base word. Now I want you to give it a try.*

- Write these words on the board:

           nesting   adds

- *I want you to find the base word in each of these words. Turn to your partner and say, I found the base word by _____.*

- Allow students enough time to share their thinking with their partner. Ask several students to share their thinking and discuss.

Guided Practice

Materials: Base Word Definition Chart

Base Word Cards

- Reproduce and cut out the base word cards provided on the PDR-CD.

- *We have learned that some words we need to know the meaning of may not be in the dictionary. We need to know the base word of the word to find its meaning.*

- Review the Base Word Definition Chart with the students.

- *I showed you how to find the base word when 's', 'ed' or ' ing' has been added to it.*

- *We are going to practice finding base words again. Then we will be ready to learn how to find unknown words in the dictionary.*

- *I am going to give you a card with a word on it. I want you to read the word to yourself and think about the base word that is in your word.*

- Pass out the base word cards. Give the students a time locate their base word.

- *Three students in the class have words with the same base word. I want you to find the students who has the same base word. When you have a group of three students with the same base words, sit on the floor together.*

- Allow students time complete the task and continue when all students are seated on the floor.

- *I am going to call a group at a time. I want you to come to the front of the class. You will read the word on your card. The rest of the class will find the base word you all had in common.*

- Allow each group to come to the front of the class and share their word cards.

- *You all did a great job in finding the base words. You have shown me that you are ready to learn how to find unknown words that have 's', 'ed', or 'ing' added to them in the dictionary.*

Shared Reading

Materials: Big Book

Chart paper / markers

- As the class is participating in shared reading, take time for the students to share words in which 's', 'ed', and 'ing' have been added to the base word.

- Write these words on chart paper and underline the base word and the endings in different color markers. This will allow the students to see just how many words have inflectional endings.

Small Group Reading

Materials: Text used in small group

Student response journals or sticky notes

- After students have completed reading their books during small group reading, have each student locate words with each of the inflectional endings: 's', 'ed', and 'ing'.
- Students write these words in their response journal or on a sticky note, and underline the base word.

Options:

- Spread this lesson over three days and ask student to locate one inflectional ending each day.
- Use this activity as a Shared Reading and make a chart of the words you locate during reading.

Independent Reading

Materials: Texts on independent reading levels

Student response journals

- Ask students to make 3 columns in their response journal.
- Place 's' at the top of one column, 'ed' at the top of the middle column, and 'ing' at the top of the last column.
- As the students are reading at their independent reading level, have them locate words with the inflectional endings: 's', 'ed', and 'ing'.
- Students write the words under the correct heading and underline the base word.

Option: Provide a worksheet with these headings at the top in a station and provide several levels of books or books from small groups. Students work in this station to locate words with one of the inflectional endings or all three and list them under each column.

A Step Beyond

- Provide a list of words in which the inflectional endings of 's', 'ed', and 'ing' have been added.
- The students find the base word, locate the word in the dictionary, select one of the definitions, and use the original word in a sentence of their own.

Example: bats

Tom <u>bats</u> at baseball practice when it is his turn.

- Have a word of the week. Place the word on the board on Monday and talk about it during the week.

Monday	Locate the base word
Tuesday	Discuss if the base word is a noun or verb
Wednesday	Talk about the different of the word

Thursday	Locate the base word in the dictionary and determine if there are additional/different meanings of the word
Friday	Use the word in an original sentence

Base Word
Across the Curriculum

Math	Use glossary
Science	or dictionary
Social Studies	when encountering
Other	unknown words

Best Definition
Dictionary, Glossary

Best Definition, Dictionary, Glossary

Teacher Talk

What: (What is the best definition?): Sometimes words have several meanings. The words and sentences around the unknown word can give clues. Sometimes they are found close to the new word. Sometimes the reader must look in the paragraph before or after the word. Use information provided in the text and what makes sense to choose the best definition. Example: He put the groceries in the <u>bag</u>.

Choices: sack, purse, used as a bed or base (baseball)

The best definition for bag as it is used in the sentence is sack. The other choices don't make sense in the context of the reading.

Why: (Why does it help you as a reader?): The glossary or dictionary will give you the meaning of the unknown word. If there is more than one definition, you select the one that makes the most sense.

When: (When is it used during reading?): You can go to a glossary or dictionary anytime you don't understanding what the author is saying and you can't find any context clues to help you.

What does research tell us about this strategy?

"To be most effective, vocabulary instruction should include multiple encounters with words in varied contexts and engagement in active processing of word meanings."

McKeown, M.G. (1993). Creating effective definitions for young word learners. *Reading Research Quarterly, 28*(1). P. 16-31.

What is expected at this level when using the strategy?

The glossaries in the first grade science, social studies, and health text are easier to use than the beginning dictionaries. The use of the glossary should be modeled and practiced before the use of the dictionary.

What prior knowledge or schema do the students need to have?

Children must be reading at the instructional level of the glossary or dictionary if they are expected to use the references. The ability to use context clues is needed if more than one definition is shared in the dictionary entry.

What are the cautions and tips when teaching this strategy?

- Students must know their alphabet and alphabetical order before being ready to use a glossary or beginning dictionary to look up an unknown word.

- Glossaries in the back of content area texts are usually easier to use than beginning dictionaries. Begin with glossaries and then move on to the beginning dictionaries.

- Dictionary skills are introduced in first grade. Kindergartners usually are not ready for this skill. If a teacher chooses, she may introduce the skill and model it using a big book with a glossary. Many students may not master this skill at this level.

- Leave the beginning dictionaries out for the students to browse through and explore during free time. Some children love to read the dictionary. It will also give you an opportunity to observe the students and where they are in their dictionary skills.

- Many students will have trouble finding words in the dictionary. Students should work in pairs with another student that has mastered the skill.

- Kindergarten children are not expected to use these reference materials. Introduce and model during shared reading with a big book to provide exposure for students who may be reading at higher levels in Kindergarten.

Expectations

Best Definition, Dictionary, Glossary			
Grade Introduced – I Grade Developed – D	K	1	2
Reading		I	D
Writing			I

Best Definition

Introduction

Materials: Best Definition Chart

- Prepare and display the Best Definition Chart shown below. A blackline master is also provided on the PDR-CD. The teacher should enlarge the chart, create their own example of the chart, or make a transparency to show the students.

- Use the definition chart to introduce the strategy. Name and define the strategy, including why and when to use the strategy during reading. (Refer to Teacher Talk)

Best Definition

Words can mean more than one thing. Use 'context clues' around the word to select the best definition.

The boy hit the ball with the <u>bat</u>.

Display and review the Definition Chart. **Think aloud** and explain the definition to the students. Use familiar books to illustrate the definition.

- Use think aloud talk to explain the definition to the students. Be sure they understand that sometimes context clues alone will not help you know the meaning of the word.

- When discussing the definition and key phrases use an example of a situation or familiar book to activate prior knowledge about the strategy.

Model

Activity 1

Materials: Best Definition Chart
Social Studies or Science text with a glossary

- Review the Best Definition chart with the students.

- *Select a page from the text that contains a word the students may not know but is in the glossary.*

- ***You will be learning many new things this year. In order to select the best definition that fits a word, you must be able to use a glossary or dictionary.***

- ***Today I will use a glossary to help me find the definition or meaning of a word. A glossary can be found in the back of a book.***

- Turn in the science or social studies text to the glossary.
- *It has a list of words that are found in the text that a reader may not know.*
- Turn to the text and read the marked selection you have selected.
- *I am not sure what the word _____ means in this sentence. But I do know the glossary can help me.*
- Turn to the glossary and use think aloud to model how you found that part in the book.
- *It is a good thing that I know my alphabet. The words in the glossary are listed in ABC order. That makes it easier for me to find the word I am looking for.*
- Point to the letters at the top of a page and explain that the word you are searching for will be found under its beginning letter.
- *I am looking for the word _____so I will find the words that begin with _____. Some glossaries have two columns of words and you search by moving down the first column and then up to the top of the next column.*
- If your dictionary contains columns model how to use them.
- Share your word, where you found it, and any information you find. There may be a picture, a sentence, and a definition. Sometimes there is a page number where the word is found in the text.
- Find that page and search and point out your word. The sentence by the word in the glossary may be the same sentence you read by the glossary entry. Let the children know if that is true.
- *Now I understand the meaning of my word and I can understand the text.*
- *Repeat this process at least two more times to model for the students.*
- *Now, it is your turn to find some words in the glossary. List three or four words on the board that are found in the glossary. Work with your partner and locate the words I have written on the board in the glossary.*
- Pass out the books and have the students find their words in the glossary.
- Students can work with partners or independently.
- Ask students to stop to talk about how they found the word and what information they were given.
- *Now that you have found your word in the glossary I want you turn to your partner and say: The way I found the word _____ was_____.*
- Allow students enough time to share their thinking with their partner. Ask several students to share their thinking and discuss.
- Possible sentences from two glossaries:
- HARCOURT SCIENCE, Grade 1. "Everything around you is called matter." The

entry for matter includes a picture, the word in a yellow box, and the page number where the word is found in the text. This glossary uses a two-column format.

- SOCIAL STUDIES, All Together, Grade 1, Scott Foresman. "The farmer grows goods such as fruit and vegetables." This glossary also includes pictures, sentences, and page numbers. The sentence in the glossary is not the same as the sentence inside the text. This glossary uses a one-column format.

Activity 2

> Materials: Best Definition Chart
> Beginning dictionaries (one for two or three students)

- Before this modeling is done, the children should be able to alphabetize using second letters of words and understand what letters come at the beginning, middle, and end of the alphabet.

- Review the Best Definition Chart with the students.

- ***I know how to use a glossary to find the best definition of a word. Today, I am going to use a dictionary. A dictionary is larger and has more pages than the glossary. It is a book all by itself and not a book inside another book. I will have to work harder to find the word that I need, but I will use the same skills I used before. I need to know the alphabet and the spelling of the word I am going to find.***

- Make a chart showing the guide words. Share the parts of the dictionary and locate the guide words.

- ***The guide words make it easier for me to find the word I am looking for.***

- Think aloud and demonstrate that the first guide word is the first word on the page and the second is the last word.

- ***Today I want to find the best definition for the word _____ in this sentence.***

- Write the sentence from a familiar text you selected on the board. Make sure the word is in the beginning dictionary you are using.

- Model finding the word for the students. Use think aloud as you use the skills to find the word.

- Read the definitions aloud and choose the best meaning for your unknown word. Continue to think aloud as you model for the students.

- ***I want you to take some time and explore the dictionary. We will work more with locating words in the dictionary later.***

- Pass out dictionaries to the students and let them explore. Have them **stop to talk** about what they see and notice.

- Model finding the best definition in the dictionary with two more words.

- ***Now I want you to give it a try. I am going to write a word on the board and***

I want you to work with your partner and find the word in your dictionary. Remember what you need to do to find the word. Let's review before you start. Review the procedure you demonstrated earlier.

- Allow students time to work together to locate the word. If students need help work together as a class to locate the word.

- Ask several students to share how they located the word.

Guided Practice

Materials: Best Definition Chart

Beginning dictionaries

- Review the Best Definition Chart with the students.

- *I have shown you how I can use a dictionary to find the meanings of words. Now, I will show you how to find the best definition of a word that has more than one meaning.*

- Review with the students the steps you took to find the word in the dictionary. Review using the alphabet and guide words.

- *You have explored the dictionary, and today I want you to try to find the best definition of a word by using a dictionary.*

- Write a sentence on the board and underline the word you want the students to find the best definition for. Read the sentence for the students. *I want you to work in small groups and find the best definition for the word _____.*

- This is a difficult skill for many first graders. Model the steps below by locating a word in the dictionary. Next, guide the students by asking them to break it down into steps:

- *Find the part of the dictionary where words are located that begin like the word _____.*

- *Use the guide words to help you find the page the word is located on*

- *Find the word itself*

- *Read the definitions*

- When all students have found the word, have them read the definition or definitions.

- *Which definition is the best fit for our word in the sentence on the board? Why? Were there context clues in the sentence that helped you find the best definition? What were they?*

- Write a new sentence on the board that contains a word you know is in the dictionaries they are using.

- Have them continue to work as a group using their alphabetical knowledge and the guide words.

Story Structure

Main Idea
and
Supporting Details

Main Idea and Supporting Details

Teacher Talk

What: (What is the main idea and supporting details?) The main idea of the text is what the text is mostly about. Sometimes the writer tells you the main idea directly. Sometimes the writer suggests the main idea from information given in the text, and you must put in together.

The supporting details are small bits of information stated in the text that help define and give more information about the main idea. They often tell who, what, where, when, why and how. Not all of these are necessary to identify the main idea but can be interchanged according to which detail is supported by the text.

Why: (Why does it help you as a reader?) The main idea helps the reader identify the gist of the text. Supporting details are used by the reader to determine the main idea.

When: (When is it used during reading?) Readers use main idea, and supporting details when they read a selection, combine the parts of the text, then use the information to form one main thought.

What does research tell us about this strategy?
Leading reading authorities Fountas and Pinnell (2000), citing research based on a 1984 Baumann study, have stated, "To comprehend, a reader must continually construct meaning while processing an extended text. Readers keep the meaning of the whole text in mind, and this process varies with the kind of texts they read."

What is expected at this level when using the strategy?
Readers at this level are introduced to connecting ideas and themes across texts during reading; and generate ideas for topics for writing.

What prior knowledge or schema do the students need to have?
Understanding that the authors have a message they are telling in their story and the main idea is what the story is mostly about.

What are the cautions and tips when teaching this strategy?

- This strategy is complex and should be introduced and model with familiar text.

- When introducing this strategy, especially with younger readers, a text that has a strong central main idea is best. For example, using a text that focuses on one main event (i.e. going to the circus, the first day of school, meeting a new friend, etc.). Pictures can also be used to introduce the strategy. Students focus on finding the main idea of a picture that may have many smaller elements.

Expectations

Main Idea and Supporting Details			
Grade Introduced – I **Grade Developed - D**	**K**	**1**	**2**
Reading		I	D
Writing	I	D	D

Main Idea and Supporting Details

Introduction

Materials: Main Idea and Supporting Details Definition Chart
Main Idea Picture of Circus Transparency
Supporting Details Picture of Circus Transparency

- Prepare and display the Main Idea and Supporting Details Definition Chart shown below. A blackline master is also provided on the PDR-CD. The teacher should enlarge the chart, create their own example of the chart, or make a transparency to show the students.

- Use the definition chart to introduce the strategy. Name and define the strategy, including why and when to use the strategy during reading. (Refer to Teacher Talk)

- Make transparencies of the main idea picture of the circus and the supporting

---

Main Idea

The **main idea** is what the story is mainly about.

The **supporting details** often tell who, what, when, where, why, and how.

Main Idea - Pizza

Details

Key Phrases
- I can see from the picture that …
- The main idea of the picture is …
- The details that helped me decide what the main idea is …

---

details picture of the circus that are provided at the end of the unit.

- First, place the main idea transparency on the overhead. Explain that by looking at the picture you can tell what is happening. Discuss what parts of the picture let you know that a boy and girl are at the circus.

- *I know the main idea of the picture is that a boy and girl are at the circus.*

- Next, place the supporting details transparency on top of the main idea transparency.

- Share with the students how the details of the new picture have added to your understanding of what the boy and girl are experiencing at the circus.

- *These details add to the picture and tell me more about the main idea. All of these details support my thinking that the main idea of the picture is a boy and girl at the circus.*

Model

Activity 1

Materials: Main Idea and Supporting Details Definition Chart
4 pictures (simple main idea) from picture books for modeling

- Review the Main Idea and Supporting Details Definition Chart with the students.
- Select a picture from a picture book to show the students and think aloud about the main idea or what the picture is mostly about. Continue to think aloud and name the important details in the picture.
- Repeat this process two more times as a model for the students using different pictures.
- Now, show the students another picture that was chosen ahead of time.
- ***This time I want you to give it a try. Look closely at all the details in the picture.***
- Allow students enough time to look at the picture.
- ***Now stop to talk to your partner about the main ideas of the picture. Turn to your partner and say, The main idea of the picture is _____.***

  The teacher may need to repeat this process several different times using other picture books.

Activity 2

> Materials: 4 familiar Big Books or Picture Books

- Select a familiar book that the students have heard read multiple times. Use think aloud to discuss how to find the main idea and supporting details in an entire story.
- ***Since I have read this book before, I need to think about the supporting details. I know from the text that _____.***
- Talk about the supporting details. During the modeling be sure to name some of the important details in the story and tell who, what, when, where, why, and how.
- ***I think this story is mostly about _____. That is the main idea of the story. I can find out the main idea from the pictures and words in a story. These are supporting details.***
- Repeat this process at least 2 more times using other familiar big books or picture books.

Activity 3

> Materials: Main Idea and Supporting Details Chart
>   4 familiar Big Books or Picture Books
>   Chart paper with a hand outlined and marker

- Make a chart or transparency with the outline of a hand on it to use later in the lesson.
- Talk to the students about how their fingers are connected to the palm of their hand. Have them examine their hands and move their fingers to reinforce this concept.
- ***The main idea and supporting details of a story are connected together as well.***
- Show them the hand you have drawn.

- *The palm of the hand is like the main idea. The fingers are like the supporting details.*
- Write the main idea of one of the familiar stories that you read in Activity 2 to the students on the palm of the hand.
- Review the supporting details from the same story. Write a supporting detail on each of the fingers as you say them.
- *The fingers often refer to the who, what, when, where, and why. You can refer to your hand when thinking about the main idea and supporting details.*
- Repeat this process at least 2 more times using the other familiar big books and picture books from Activity 2.
- Now you are ready to ask students stop to talk to a partner about the who, what, when, where, and why of a familiar story they have read.
- *Now it's your turn to give it a try. Turn to your partner and say: The supporting details are _____.*
- Allow students enough time to share their thinking with their partner. Ask several students to share their thinking and discuss.

Guided Practice

Materials: Various picture books with Main Idea and Supporting Details
Teacher selected text for Read Aloud - 4 possible titles for text
Drawing paper, pencils and crayons

- Before the lesson, cover the front of the picture book you have chosen to read aloud. Write down four possible titles that could fit the text.
- *Today I will read you a story without telling you the title. Your job is to choose a title for the book and design a picture for your cover.*
- Before reading the story, share the four possible titles for the book. Guide the students in listening for the details in the story to help them choose the correct title.
- Read the book aloud to the students.
- *Now that you have heard the story, which title do you think best fits the story? Why?*
- They should be able to use supporting details to back up their responses.
- Ask students to write the title that they chose on a piece of paper and draw a picture to match it. Allow time for the students to share their pictures with one another.
- Use various picture books to discuss how the pictures (supporting details) may be different but the titles (main idea) are all the same.
- The teacher may choose to use these to hang these papers to create a Main Idea and Supporting Details bulletin board.

Activity 2

Materials: Nursery rhyme cutouts (PRD-CD)
Ziploc baggies

- Before the lesson, print out the nursery rhymes provided at the end of the unit, and cut them apart. Place each nursery rhyme in a separate baggie.
- Write out <u>Hickory Dickory Dock (shown below)</u> onto sentence strips.

   Each line should go on a separate strip:

> Hickory, Dickory, Dock
>
> The mouse ran up the clock.
>
> The clock struck one,
>
> Down he did run,
>
> Hickory, Dickory, Dock.

- Review with the students their prior learning about main idea and supporting details. Tell them that these strategies for understanding text are used not only in pictures and stories but also in nursery rhymes.
- Place the sentence strips for Hickory, Dickory, Dock out of order on the board.
- Use think aloud talk as you read the sentence strips and tell the students that they are not in the correct order. Place them in the order they should be. Read the nursery rhyme aloud. *I think aloud about the main idea of this rhyme is that a mouse ran up a clock.*
- Point to that sentence strip. *Do the other details tell about what happened when the mouse ran up the clock?*
- Point to the other strips and think aloud about the details you see. *I now know my thinking is correct.*
- Divide the students into small groups. Give each group a bag with a nursery rhyme. Explain to the students that they are going to read each of the strips. They are to place them in order. They will then find the strip that tells them the main idea of the nursery rhyme. They will check to see if the other strips are supporting details.
- Allow time for the students to share their nursery rhymes and discuss the main idea and supporting details.

Options:

- Provide a copy of the nursery rhyme for those groups that need more support reading the rhyme independently.
- Work together to put the nursery rhymes together and discuss.

Shared Reading

> Materials: Big Book
>   Student response journals

- Read a big book along with the students. Take time to let the students discuss supporting details as the story is read.
- Ask each of the students to write the main idea of the story in their response journal and draw a picture that shows the main idea along with the supporting details.

Small Group Reading

> Materials: Texts used in small reading groups
>   Student response journals

- Guide the students as they read their book. Give the students the opportunity to reread their book several times.
- Ask the students trace their hand in their response journal. Refer to the chart with the hand that you used earlier to model main idea and supporting details.
- Ask them write the main idea in the palm of their hand and a supporting detail on each finger.

Read Aloud – Multiple Strategy Practice

> Materials: New Picture Books for Read Aloud
>   4-5 Introduced strategies for practice

- As new strategies are introduced, it is important to continue to practice previously introduced strategies and orchestrate them with the new strategy. Choose 3-4 strategies that have been introduced in previous lessons to review and practice with the new strategy.
- Set up the read aloud by selecting appropriate places to stop in the text to practice the strategies selected. Prepare a sticky note for each strategy writing a key phrase for the strategy to be practiced. The sticky notes are placed on the page as a signal as you read to stop and ask the students to turn to their partner and practice the strategy. Example: ***Turn to your partner and say, I predict …and tell you partner what you predict and why.***
- Allow students enough time to share their thinking with their partner. Ask several students to share their thinking and discuss.
- Continue to read until you come to the next stopping point. Repeat practicing another selected strategy.

Note: Select texts that support the strategies for practice. Example strategies practiced could be; predicting, asking a question, describe a character, setting, and summary.

Independent Reading

Materials: Texts on independent reading levels
Wordless Picture Books may be used with non-readers

- Ask the students to read a book on their independent reading level.

- Ask each student to choose a partner. Each student shares the main idea and supporting details of their books with their partner. They may refer to their "hand" to help them if needed.

A Step Beyond

- Provide a station activity for students to practice main idea and supporting details. This station may incorporate the "connecting hand" that was modeled.

- The students trace their hand. They write a main idea sentence about themselves in the palm of the hand.

- They write a supporting detail on each finger that describes them. Use the main idea sentence and supporting details to write a paragraph about themselves.

- Provide books at the independent reading level of the students. Have them read a book and then give the book a new name. They could design a new cover for the book.

- Read various books and show the main idea and supporting details in a new way
Examples include:

  - Chrysanthemum: Make a flower. Write the main idea in the center of the flower. Write a supporting detail on each petal.

  - Curious George Flies a Kite: Make a kite. The main idea goes on the kite and the supporting details on the tail of the kite.

  - Spiders: Make a spider. The main idea goes on the body of the spider and the supporting details go on the legs.

- The students write a paragraph telling about something they are studying in science or social studies. Have them write their paper with the main idea followed by the supporting details. They may use their "hand" as a pre writing activity to guide them.

- The students write about an experience that they have had but leave out the beginning sentence or main idea. They can read the paper of a classmate and write the missing main idea sentence.

Setting

Setting

Teacher Talk

What: (What is the setting?): The setting is the time (when) and place (where) that events in the story happen. Sometimes the setting influences the lives of the characters and the plot. When the setting is not stated, look for clues like the season, the year, the time of day or the time in history. The setting is more important in some stories than others. A description of the setting helps create a picture in your mind.

Why: (Why does it help you as a reader?): The setting helps you create a mental picture. Readers use setting to help establish the place and time for the story. The setting is more important in some stories than others.

When: (When is it used during reading?) The reader must depend upon the illustrations and other clues in the story. These clues might include the season and time of year.

What does research tell us about this strategy?
According to Reading experts, Fountas and Pinnell (2000), "Analyzing literary elements such as setting helps readers see so much more in a text, especially as they reflect on and discuss their analysis with others."

What is expected at this level when using the strategy?
The students are expected to describe how illustrations contribute to the text's setting, draw and establish visual images about the setting based on text descriptions, and identify the importance of the setting to a story's meaning.

What prior knowledge or schema do the students need to have?

- Students should master using illustrations to find the setting before teaching using the text.

- Use examples of personal experiences to connect the term setting to school settings, home settings, and community settings.

What are the cautions and tips when teaching this strategy?

- Students need prior knowledge about settings in order to make connections.

- Some stories have multiple settings. Students need guidance if one setting is to be chosen as the main setting. This setting would be the setting where most of the story happened.

    Example: <u>Jack</u> <u>and</u> <u>the</u> <u>Beanstalk</u>

    Jack's home, market, beanstalk, Giant's castle

    Main Setting: Giant's Castle.

Expectations

Setting			
Grade Introduced – I Grade Developed - D	K	1	2
Reading	I	D	D
Writing		I	D

Setting

Introduction

Materials: Setting Definition Chart
Pictures or scenes from books that show different settings

- Prepare and display the Setting Definition Chart shown below. A blackline master is also provided on the PDR-CD. Teachers should enlarge the chart, create their own example of the chart, or make a transparency to show the students.

- Use the definition chart to introduce the strategy. Name and define the strategy, including why and when to use the strategy during reading. (Refer to Teacher Talk)

Setting
The setting is the time (when) and place (where) that the events in the story happen.

Key Phrases
- The setting of the story is _____because_____.
- The setting reminds me of _____.
- The picture I see in my mind is _____.

- Display the Setting Definition Chart.
- When discussing the definition and key phrases use an example of a situation or familiar book to activate prior knowledge about the strategy prediction.
- ***When we read stories we think about where and when the story happened. We can use pictures, characters, and words in the story to help us know the setting.***
- Display one of the pictures. Examples: The moon shining would mean it was night time, the barn with cows and chickens tells us the story is at a farm, the beach and sun could tell us it is hot and it is summer. ***Knowing the setting helps to create a picture in our mind, Then it becomes easier to make connections and remember the story.***

Model

Materials: Setting Definition Chart
3-5 pictures showing different settings for discussion

- ***Yesterday, we talked about the setting of stories. We discussed looking at pictures and words in the story to help us know where the story takes place. Let's look at our chart about settings and read it again. Today we are going to talk about how pictures give us clues about the setting. The first thing we do when we read is to look at the pictures on the cover of the book. We can look at the pictures on the cover and make predictions about the setting of the story.***
- Display the cover of a book. Think aloud and model what you notice on the cover

that gives you clues about the setting. Model using the key phrases listed above.

Look for clues in the picture that tell where and when the event is happening. Close your eyes and think aloud to make connections to sounds, smells, and feelings with the setting. If you are showing a picture of the beach, then discuss the sun, the sky, how the sand feels under your toes, and the sound of the waves as they rush to shore, the taste of the salt water, etc. Remember to give evidence for your thinking.

- Repeat this process at least 2 more times using other pictures of settings.
- Display another book or picture and ask the students to **stop to talk** to their partner.
- ***Turn to your partner and say, The setting of the story is _____ because_____.***
- Allow students enough time to share their thinking with their partner. Ask several students to share their thinking and discuss.

Activity 2

> Materials: Text containing 3-5 places to model setting
> Setting Definition Chart

- Preview the book and locate good places to stop and model how words can give us clues about the setting. Place a sticky note on those pages and write what you are going to model using key phrases to start your talk.
- ***The last few days we have been talking about how we use pictures and clues in stories to know the setting. Yesterday I modeled for you how we use pictures to know the setting, and today I am going to model using words in the story to make a picture in your mind about the setting.***
- Review the Setting Definition Chart.
- ***Today I am going to read a story to you and I am going to show you how the words help me make a picture in my mind about the setting.*** Use think aloud to model how words can give us clues to the setting. Read aloud and stop at the pre-selected stopping points. Model by reading the description of the setting and then discussing the picture you have in your mind.
- ***The picture I see in my mind is _____. The words in the text that helped me are _____.***
- Repeat modeling at pre-selected stopping points.
- ***Now I want you to give it a try. I am going to read about another setting. This time I want you to close your eyes as I read and make a picture of the setting in your mind. Listen carefully to the words and how they tell you about the setting of the story.***
- Read the text and give students time to think about the setting, making a picture in their minds.
- ***Turn to your partner and say, The picture I see in my mind is _____ because _____.***

- Allow students just enough time to discuss the pictures in their mind. Ask students to wind up their talk, and allow several students to share.
- Make a chart and list the clues from the text that helped the students make a picture in their minds. Discuss how different words can give us different clues. Discuss how putting the illustrations and words together help us know the setting.

Option: Display the pictures from the text you just read to the students, and discuss which gave you more clues to the setting.

Activity 3

Materials: 3-4 familiar texts including setting central to the story meaning
Setting Definition Chart

- *For the last few days we talked about the setting of a story and how pictures and words can help us to know the setting. Many times the setting is important because of where and when things happen in the story. Today I am going to model my thinking about how the setting affects the story using stories you know.*

- Think aloud to model the setting and the importance to the story's meaning. Stop at pre-selected stopping points and model using key phrases. *The setting of the story was _____. I know the setting was important to the story because _____. I wonder if the setting was changed, would the same thing happen. Could the same thing happen if the setting had been _____ instead of _____? I know the story happened in the _____. Could the story have happened in _____? I think that the setting is very important to the meaning of the story.*

- Repeat modeling at pre-selected stopping points.

- *Now I want you to give it a try. I want you to think about the story of The Three Little Pigs. Think about changing the setting from the woods to a big city, the North Pole, or the desert. Turn to your partner and say, I think the setting was important to the story because _____.*

- Allow students just enough time to discuss. Ask students to wind up their talk, and allow several students to share. Repeat this with other stories if time, such as Little Red Riding Hood, etc.

Guided Practice
Activity 1

Materials: Pictures of various settings or texts for small group reading
Setting Definition Chart

- *For the last few days I have been modeling for you how I use words and pictures to know the setting of stories. We have also talked about how the setting is important to the things that happen in the story.*

- Review Setting Definition Chart.

Option: This activity can be done in small group reading with instructional level text. After completing your guided reading lesson, ask the students to turn to their partner and talk about the setting of the story and explain their thinking. Allow students to share.

- *Today I am going to show you pictures of characters and setting. I want you to talk to your partner about the characters, the setting, and what is happening in the picture. Remember to talk about the clues that helped you. Turn to your partner and say, I think _____. I think this because_____.*

Option: This can be done as separate activities. Discuss characters, then setting and what is happening.

- Divide the students into small groups, and give each group a picture for discussion.
- Students look at the picture and work together to find as many clues as they can to discuss the setting and what is happening.
- Sit in on small groups, and use the following questions to focus their talk if needed.
- Allow students just enough time to discuss. Ask students to wind up their talk, and allow several students to share their picture and their findings.

Activity 2

Materials: Setting Definition Chart
"Setting" writings (PDR-CD)
"Setting Created by Text" (PDR-CD)
Text (mark the part of the text that describes the setting)

- *The past few day we a have talked about clues in stories that help us decide the time and place of the setting. Today I am going to read a story to you, and I want you to tune in and listen for clues that help you know the setting as I read. I will do the first one for you.*

- Select one of the setting paragraphs to read aloud. Model using think aloud, and discuss how you know the setting and the clues that helped.

- *This time I want give it a try.* Read the next short paragraph aloud. *Turn to your partner and say, I think the setting was _____ because _____.*

- Allow students just enough time to discuss. Ask students to wind up their talk, and allow several students to share.

- Repeat as necessary.

Option: Chart the setting for each paragraph and the clues that helped identify when and where the story took place.

Settings	Clues

Activity 3

Materials: Setting Definition Chart
Familiar text from different places and periods appropriate for young students
Story / Change Chart (PDR-CD)
Student response journals

Suggestions for texts include:

- A story that happened long ago
- A story that happens in the forest
- A story that happens at the zoo
- A story that happens in the future

- *We have talked about the setting of the story <u>The Three Little Pigs</u> and how the setting was important to the story. If we changed the setting of <u>The Three Little Pigs</u> to the city, do you think the story would have been the same? Today we are going to look at books we have been reading this year and change something about the story. For example: If <u>Little Red Riding Hood</u> happened in the city instead of the woods, Grandma would have been safe because wolves do not live in the city.*

  Questions to focus talk:

- Who or What would change?
- Would the characters have to change?
- Would the story have to change?
- Explain to the students that they are going to change the story in some way. The setting may stay the same but the characters would change to characters that normally would not be in this setting. Or, the characters may stay the same but the setting is changed to make the story completely different.
- Review each story and allow the students time to **stop to talk** with their partner and think of a way to change the story.
- Allow students just enough time to discuss the story, and allow students to share their thinking.
- Use the chart below to write down how students decided to change the story.
- Repeat this activity for the stories selected. Ask students to choose one of the stories, and draw or write their story with changes in their student response journal.

Story	Change

Independent Practice

Activity 1

Materials: Familiar Big Book, Picture Book, Wordless Picture Books
Student response journals

• *Today as you read in partnership reading or reading stations, I want you to use sticky notes to mark places in the book that gave you clues about the setting.*

• *Talk to your partner about the setting, and then draw in your student response journal the clues you found in the book that helped you know the setting.*

Activity 2

Materials: Texts used in small group instruction
Student response journals

• *Today as you read in partnership reading or reading stations, I want you to reread books from your book box and talk to your partner about the setting.*

• *Then draw a picture of the setting in your student response journal. Label the setting or write a sentence telling about the setting.*

A Step Beyond

• Provide pictures with settings of different seasons and times of the day. Students sort the picture by the season or the time of day.

• Provide a station activity for students to practice finding the setting of a story. Be sure the station has a variety of books with many different settings. Have a chart that lists the different settings with picture codes. (sun, moon, home, school, zoo) Have the students make tally marks by the setting for the book.

• Ask students read two books with the same setting. They may then write in their response journals how the stories were alike and different.

• Ask students rewrite a story by placing themselves in the story. They must remember that their actions depend upon the setting of the story they are rewriting.

• Ask students read a text with multiple settings. Have them draw the different settings in their response journal. They may then find and circle the main setting.

• Select a short fiction and non-fiction text with an unidentified setting. Cover the setting information in the text with tape or post it notes. Students must use the clues in the pictures to help determine the time and place the story took place. They must be able to tell how they found the setting of the story.

Setting
Across the Curriculum

Math	• Time (am and pm) – using the clock
Science	• Discuss the "setting" for a lab or experiment • Connect "setting" to habitats
Social Studies	• Tie in with geography • Discuss settings when discussing eras of history. (Colonial times, etc.) • Neighborhood, city, state, country, continent
Other	• Art: Discuss the settings in prints • Music: Identify settings of songs. Example "Over in the Meadow", "Texas, Our Texas"

Character Traits
Emotions
Motives

Character Traits

Teacher Talk

What: (What are character traits, emotions and motives?): Characters are the people or animals in a story. When looking at characters, notice details about how they look, feel and act. The details that tell about their personalities are called character traits. Identifying and understanding characters' traits, emotions and motives help the reader understand the characters.

Why: (How does it help you as a reader?): Knowing about the character helps the reader understand the story better by making personal connections with the characters.

When: (When is it used during reading?) When you want to understand a character and their behavior, you look for details about the character in the text.

What does research tell us about this strategy?
"Student responses to character development are important." Taylor, B (2002, July) "Readers who are unaware of structure do not approach a text with any particular plan of action (Meyer, Brandt, & Bluth, 1980). Consequently, they tend to retrieve information in a seemingly random way. Students who are aware of text structure organize the text as they read, and they recognize and retain the important information it contains." A Research Agenda for Improving Reading Comprehension, RAND Reading Study Group, p. 40, 2002

What is expected at this level when using the strategy?
Students discuss and present dramatic interpretations of character traits, feelings, relationships and changes.

What prior knowledge or schema do the students need to have?
- Ability to recognize supporting details
- Some knowledge of story elements and how they unfold in the story.

What are the cautions and tips when teaching this strategy?
- Students usually find it easier to find the character trait before identifying the character motive.
- The word labels for emotions must be a part of the student's listening and speaking vocabulary.
- Students make personal connections to analyze character traits.
- The text must be an appropriate reading level to enable students to search the text for information to support their thinking.

Expectations

Character Traits, Emotions, Motives			
Grade Introduced – I Grade Developed – D	K	1	2
Reading		I	D
Writing		I	D

Character Traits, Emotions, Motives

Introduction

Material: Character Traits Definition Chart

- Prepare and display the Character Traits Definition Chart shown below. A blackline master is also provided on the PDR-CD. The teacher should enlarge the chart, create their own example of the chart, or make a transparency to show the students.

- Use the definition chart to introduce the strategy. Name and define the strategy, including why and when to use the strategy during reading. (Refer to Teacher Talk)

Character Traits

Character traits tell or show you how the characters (people or animals) in the story look, feel, and act.

Think about...
- how a character looks.
- what character says or thinks.
- what the character does.
- how the character feels.

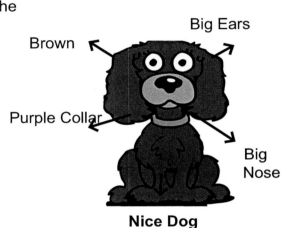

Brown

Big Ears

Purple Collar

Big Nose

Nice Dog

Key Phrases
- The characters in the story were _____.

- Display and review the Definition Chart.

- When discussing the definition and key phrases use an example of a situation or familiar book to activate prior knowledge about the strategy prediction.

Model

Materials: Character Traits Definition Chart
4 pictures from text that provides character traits such as: looks, facial expressions, body language, etc

- Review the Character Traits Definition Chart with the students.

- *I now know that how a character looks and feels helps me understand a story better. Sometimes I can get information about a character from a picture.*

- Hold up the first picture you chose to share with the students.

- *I am going to see if I can tell anything about the character in this picture by the clues I see in the picture.*

- Think aloud to model for the students. Be sure to include the physical appearance, facial expressions, and body language of the character. Some pictures may have the characters doing an action that tells you something about the character. There may be another character that tells you something about the main character in the picture you are modeling. *This picture did tell me a lot about the character. What I learned about the character helps me better understand the whole picture.*

- Repeat this process at least 2 more times using the other pictures of characters you have chosen.

- *Now I want you to give it a try.* Hold up the last picture you chose to share with the students.

- *Look at the character in this picture. Take a minute and think about what the picture tells you about this character.*

- After the students have had a minute to think about the character's traits, ask students to turn to a partner and **stop to talk**.

- *Turn to your partner and say, I think _____ was _____ because _____.*

- Allow students just enough time to complete their talk. Ask several students to share with the class what they shared with their partner.

Activity 2

Materials: Character Traits Definition Chart
Picture book including 3-5 opportunities to model character traits

- Select 3-5 appropriate places to stop in the text to model character traits using think aloud.

- Before reading aloud use sticky notes to mark stopping points in the text to model character traits. Also, choose a picture from the text that will provide evidence of the traits of the character for discussion.

- *I have learned that pictures can tell me about a character. Look at the character in one of the pages of this book.* Discuss the traits observed in the picture. Use the character trait key phrases from the definition chart when you are modeling.

- *Today as I read, listen closely for the character traits that tell us about the character.*

- *Turn to your partner and say, I think _____ was _____ because _____.*

- Allow student just long enough to share character traits. Ask students to wind up their talk, and allow several students to share character traits they discussed with their partners.

- *Pictures can give us information about a character, and now we know that words tell us about a character too. Words can tell us how a character acts and why they feel the way they do. Ask student to share new traits they know after reading the text.*

Activity 3

Materials: Character Traits Definition Chart
The Three Little Pigs 3-5 opportunities to model character traits

- If students are not familiar with the story of <u>The Three Little Pigs</u>, use another story that is familiar to students for the next part of this activity.

- Link the lesson by reviewing how pictures and words can give us information about character traits.

- ***Now I want you to think about a character you all know.*** Ask students *to close their eyes.* ***Think about the story of the three little pigs that you have heard read to you many times. Think about the third little pig. In your mind, think about what the third little pig did in the story. What did he build his house out of? Did it take him longer than the other two pigs to build his house? When the wolf blew down the houses of the first and second little pig, what did the third little pig do? After thinking about the third little pig, what do you know about him?***

- *After the students have had a few seconds to think, have them stop to talk with their partner.* ***Turn to your partner and say, I think the third little pig was _____ because _____.***

- *Allow students only enough time to complete their talk. Ask students to wind up their talk, and allow a few students to share what they know about the third little pig. (He was smart. He was a hard worker. He was caring because he shared his house with the other two little pigs.) Have students provide evidence for their thinking.*

- *Repeat this activity using little pigs 1, 2 and the wolf.*

Guided Practice

Activity 1
Materials: Text with one main character
Character Trait Graphic Organizer Chart (PDR-CD)

- ***We can learn about a character by pictures and words in the text. Today I am going to share with you an easy way of writing down the traits of a character. You will use this graphic organizer later on. It can help you organize the information you have learned about the character. You might use the information to draw a conclusion about a character or to organize your thoughts before writing about a character.***

- Display the Character Trait Graphic Organizer Chart and selected text for reading.

- ***As we look at the web we can write the name of the character we want to know about in the middle of the web.*** Write the name of the character in the middle of the web.

- **After reading our story, we will write character traits about _____ on each spoke of the web. As I read the story, listen closely to learn about _____.**

- Read the story.

- Refer back to the web. Ask students to turn and **stop to talk** with their partner. ***Turn to your partner and say, I think _____ was _____ because _____.***

- Allow students just long enough to complete their talk. Ask student to share their thinking. As they share, write their responses on the spokes of the web. Have the students give evidence to support their thinking.

- ***Now I want you to stop to talk about the character traits. Turn to your partner and say, I think _____ looks _____.*** Ask a few students to share and prove their thinking.

- Repeat using the key phrases below.

> ***I think____ feels _____.***
>
> ***I think ____ acted like ____.***
>
> ***I have/have not felt like _____.***

Activity 2

> Materials: Character Traits and Evidence Graphic Organizer Chart (PDR-CD)
> Text – <u>The Three Little Pigs</u> or Familiar Text

- ***Yesterday we used a web to help us organize our thoughts about a character. You found evidence to prove your thinking about the character. Today we are going to write what we know about the character or their traits, and write the evidence to prove our thinking.***

- Display the Character Traits and Evidence Graphic Organizer Chart and explain to students which character they will focus on today.

- ***We will use the Big Bad Wolf from the Three Little Pigs as our character. It is our job to come up with evidence to prove that the Big Bad Wolf is truly bad and scary. Turn to your partner and say, The Big Bad Wolf was _____ because _____.***

- Allow students enough time to share their thinking with their partner. Ask several students to share their thinking and discuss.

- As the students share their thoughts, write them in the character trait boxes.

- **Now let's share how you know these traits. Discuss the evidence that proves the traits listed on the graphic organizer.**

Character Trait	<u>**Evidence**</u>
Dark brown and furry	**Have seen pictures of the Big Bad Wolf**
Likes to eat pork	**He wanted to eat the 3 little pigs and pigs are pork**
Mean	**He is not nice to animals**

- ***Do we have evidence that the Big Bad Wolf is really bad and scary? Could we convince someone that he is? Turn to your partner and say, I think the Big Bad Wolf was bad and scary because _____.***

Shared Reading

      Materials: Big book with one main character
                     Character Trait Web Graphic Organizer Chart or Handout

- ***Today as I read, I want you to tune in and think about the characters in the story. After reading the story, we are going to talk about and write the character traits on our graphic organizer.***

Note: This activity can be done as a whole class, or students may work with partners or small groups.

- Introduce the book and identify the character you will describe later. Read the story aloud. Ask students to give it a try.

- ***Turn to your partner and say, The character _____ is _____ because _____.***

- Allow students enough time to discuss the character, and then allow several students to share. Display the Character Trait Web Graphic Organizer, and demonstrate how to use the web to organize the character traits of the character that they have identified. The students may work in pairs or in small groups.

- Students may draw or write the traits they discussed with their partner. Allow time for students to share their graphic organizers when completed.

Small Group Reading

      Materials: Instructional reading level text for small group
                     Character Traits and Evidence Graphic Organizer Chart or Individual Copies

- After completing the guided reading session, ask students to think about one character in the story.

Note: The teacher may model, using think aloud, the character traits of one character or have a group discussion.

- Review the graphic organizer with the students. ***Turn to your partner and say, the character _____ was _____ because _____.***

- Allow students just enough time to discuss their character and allow several to share.

- Complete the graphic organizer as a group or as an independent activity.

Independent Practice

Activity 1

      Materials: Familiar texts with main characters on independent reading levels
                     Student response journals

- Students select a book with a character they can personally connect to.

- The students reread the book and choose a character they think is the most like them.

- The student will use their response journal to draw or write about how the character is like them and why.

Activity 2

Materials: Familiar texts with main characters on independent reading levels
Student response journals

- Students choose a book from guided practice or a big book from shared reading and reread the text. They use their student response journals to draw the graphic organizer and complete it, providing character traits for the character they chose.

- Students can draw or write their responses.

Note: This activity can be used as an independent activity each day, asking students to look at one trait at a time, how the character looks, feels, acts, etc.

A Step Beyond

- Selecr two characters from the same story or different stories, and share how they are alike and different. Use a Venn Diagram to compare the story variants.

- Use their student response journal to draw or write the character traits of their best friend and give evidence.

- Select a character from a fairy tale and share the character traits and evidence.

- Have the students pretend a new student has moved into their class. Students share character traits about their new teacher (you) and give evidence for their thinking.

- Students choose a fictional character such as Superman, Cinderella, a pirate, etc. They draw or write about their character trait and give evidence for their thinking. This can be done in their student response journal or graphic organizer. These could be displayed as a class bulletin board, "We Have the Evidence".

- Have the students take a character and see if they can change the opinion most people have of that character. For example, most students would think of Goldilocks as being a nice little girl. They may share evidence otherwise:

  - She broke into the house of the three little bears.
  - She ate their food and broke their chairs.
  - She ran away without explaining why she was there.

Character Traits / Emotions / Motives
Across the Curriculum

Math	• Discuss the characters and their traits that appear in a story problem. • Create characters out of shapes, such as a triangle, and discuss their traits.
Science	• Discuss issues such as pollution, water conservation, etc. and how people feel differently about these issues. • Discuss motives of others for protecting the environment.
Social Studies	• Discuss character traits of historical figures and how the traits influenced their behavior. Example: Abraham Lincoln
Other	• Art: Examine works of art and have students discuss character traits depicted. • Music: Listen to a composition. Have the students predict how the composer felt when composing the selection.

Plot
Story Problem
Resolution

Plot, Story Problem, Resolution

Teacher Talk

What: (What is the plot?): The plot is what happens in the story. The plot includes: a beginning where the setting, main character and problem are introduced, a middle where the character tries to solve the problem, and an end where the problem may be solved. Check DR def

Why: (Why does it help you as a reader?): Knowing the plot indicates an understanding of the story.

When: (When is it used during reading?) You use it as you monitor what is happening and determine if and how the story problem is solved.

What does research tell us about this strategy?

Stein and Glenn, in their research on story comprehension, say, "Comprehending young readers recognize the story problem and its resolution."

Stein, N. L. & Glenn, C. G. (1979). An analysis of story comprehension in elementary school children. In R. O. Freedle (Ed.), New directions in discourse processing: Vol. 2. Advances in discourse processes (pp. 53-120), Norwood, New Jersey: Ablex.

What is expected at this level when using the strategy?

Students at this level recognize the plot and the story problem(s). Kindergarten and first graders use this strategy in retelling and summaries. First graders include the strategy in stories they write.

What prior knowledge or schema do the students need to have?

They must understand the meaning of "problem and resolution". Prior knowledge of setting facilitates this task.

What are the cautions and tips when teaching this strategy?

• The child who can identify with the character can better connect with the story problem and its resolution.

• Students must be able to relate to the story problem and resolution to make connections. Example: A student that just arrived from Asia might have trouble making connections about a cowboy and his lost horse.

• Use examples of personal experiences in the school, classroom, and community setting to discuss the terms plot, story problem and resolution.

• Students should be able to identify with the setting and characters in the story and the role they have in the story's plot.

Expectations

Plot, Story Problem, Resolution			
Grade Introduced – I Grade Developed – D	K	1	2
Reading		I	D
Writing			

Plot, Story Problem, Resolution

Introduction

Materials: Plot/Story Problem/Resolution Definition Chart

- Prepare and display the Plot/Story Problem/Resolution Definition Chart shown below. A blackline master is also provided at the end of the unit. The teacher should enlarge the chart, create their own example of the chart, or make a transparency to show the students.

- Use the definition chart to introduce the strategy. Name and define the strategy, including why and when to use the strategy during reading. (Refer to Teacher Talk)

Plot, Story Problem, Resolution

The **plot** is what happens in the story.

The **problem** is what is wrong in the story. The problem may or may not be solved. If the problem is solved, that is the **resolution.**

Key Phrases

- I think the plot was _____ because_____.
- I think the problem was _____because _____.
- I think the problem was resolved when _____because _____.

- When discussing the definition and key phrases use an example of a situation or familiar book to activate prior knowledge about the strategy prediction.

- Example: ***Remember when we were at lunch last week and someone dropped their lunch tray. I think the problem was that there was food all over the floor. I think the problem was resolved when we all helped to clean up the mess on the floor.***

Model

Activity 1

Materials: Plot/Story Problem/Resolution Definition Chart
Plot/Story Problem/Resolution Pictures-Problems and Resolution only (PDR-CD)
Ziploc baggies

- Review the Plot/Story Problem/Resolution Definition Chart with the students.

- ***As I think about the plot of a story, I am really thinking about the problem and resolution in the story. Let me think about the story Cinderella.***

- ***The problem was that she worked hard and was treated unkindly by her stepmother and stepsisters.***

- *Now that is the problem. I think the resolution is that the prince fell in love with her and took her to a place where she was treated nicely. Let me think about another story.*

- *Now I am thinking about the story The Little Red Hen. Her problem was that none of the other animals wanted to help her make bread. I think she solved the problem by making the bread herself. That is the resolution.*

- Display one pair of the pictures from the Plot/Story Problem/Resolution pictures. Look at each picture and use think aloud to model how you decide which picture is the problem and which is the resolution. Use these key phrases to model your thinking. *I know the problem is _____ because _____. The resolution is _____ because _____.*

- *Now I want you to give it a try.* Place the students in small groups or pairs. Give each group a set of pictures. They are to decide which picture is the problem and which is the resolution. Walk around and help students who may need help. Also listen to the students and encourage them to use the terms problem and resolution.

Activity 2
Materials: Plot/Story Problem/Resolution Definition Chart
Plot/Story Problem/Resolution Pictures – Card Set (PDR-CD)

- Review Plot/Story Problem/Resolution using the Definition Chart.

- *Earlier I shared the problem and resolution of the story <u>Cinderella</u> with you.*

- *Today I am going to see if I can think more about the plot of the story by thinking about details that happen in the story.*

- *I already know the problem is that her stepmother and stepsisters treated Cinderella unfairly. I also know the resolution is that she married the prince and moved to the castle and was treated kindly.*

- *Today I think I can tell more about the plot by sharing other events that happened between the problem of the story and the resolution. I know that she cleaned the house all by herself. I also know her stepmother and stepsisters went to a ball and Cinderella had to stay home.*

- *She was very unhappy and her fairy godmother came to make her dreams come true. She went to the ball and danced with the Prince. The clock struck twelve and she lost her shoe when she rushed home. The Prince found the shoe and searched for the girl whom the shoe fit. The shoe fit Cinderella. They got married and moved to the castle. They lived happily ever after.*

- *All of these events add to the plot of the story. They make the story much more exciting.*

- Follow the same process with the story of <u>The Little Red Hen</u>.

- *This time I want you give it a try. I am going to give back the pictures used in our earlier lesson. You will have more pictures than before. You will have pictures of the problem, resolution, and events in the story that add to the plot.*

- Students work in small groups and pass out the sets of the Plot/Story Problem/ Resolution pictures. The students will put all of the pictures in order beginning with the problem and ending with the resolution. Walk around and help students that may be having problems. Listen as they stop to talk and encourage the use of terms such as plot, problem, and resolution.

Guided Practice

Activity 1
Materials: Teacher selected text

- *We have learned that a story has a plot. The plot of a story includes the problem, events, and resolution. We have practiced this strategy using pictures and stories that are familiar to us.*
- *Today we will practice this strategy with a story that is not as familiar to us.*
- Display the book you have chosen to read. Discuss the cover together. Read the book aloud to the students. Stop as you read the parts of the story that contain the problem, important events, and the resolution.
- Ask the students to stop to talk to their partner as you come to these parts in the story.
- *Turn to your partner and say, I think the problem in the story is _____ because _____. I think the plot in the story is _____ because _____. I think the problem was resolved when _____ because _____.*
- Allow students to share after they stop to talk for each of these key phrases.
- Discuss how the events worked together to help solve the problem of the story.
- *We just read the story _____. We have discussed it together. Now I want you to stop to talk about the story problem.*
- When the students have finished sharing the problems with one another have them stop to talk about the important events.
- When the students have finished sharing the important events with one another, have them stop to talk about the resolution.

Activity 2
Materials: Teacher selected text
                 Plot/Story Problem/Resolution Graphic Organizer Chart (PDR-CD)

- *We have learned about the plot of a story. The plot includes the problem, important events, and resolution of a story*.
- Show the graphic organizer to the students. *Today we will use a graphic organizer to help us record the problem, events, and resolution of a story.*
- Show the book you have chosen to the students. Discuss the cover of the book.
- Read the book aloud to the students.
- Refer back to the graphic organizer. Have the students tell you the name of the story. Write it on the title section of the graphic organizer.

- Have the students share the character and setting of the story. Discuss how they play an important part in the plot of the story. Write the characters and setting into the appropriate section of the graphic organizer.

- Continue this process for problem, events, and resolution. When completing the events, they may share more than three. As a class try to decide upon the three that had the most impact on the plot of the story.

- ***Today we used a graphic organizer to help us record the plot of the story we read.***

- Ask students to share what they have learned and how an organizer can help them organize their thoughts.

Shared Reading

Materials: Teacher selected text

Plot/Story Problem/Resolution Graphic Organizer (PDR-CD)

- Review the definition for the term plot. Be sure they include the problem, events, and resolution.

- Explain that after the story today, they will work in small groups to practice what they have learned.

- Read the book along with the students.

- Place the students into small groups or pairs and provide a graphic organizer.

- Explain that they are to work together in completing the graphic organizer.

- Walk around and give guidance if needed. Listen closely as the students use the new vocabulary they have learned.

Small Group Reading

Materials: Texts used in small group reading

Plot/Story Problem/Resolution Graphic Organizer

- Students reread the book they are reading in small groups.

- Have the students work together to complete the graphic organizer.

- The students will share the information with the class. They may choose who will share about the characters and setting, who will share about the problem, etc.

- If each of your small reading groups completes this activity, the class will have more opportunities to hear about the plot.

Independent Practice

Materials: Various books at independent reading levels

- Students select a book at their independent reading level. Students read the book they have selected.

- Students stop to talk about the plot of their story. They should include the problem, events and resolution.

A Step Beyond

- Provide the plot/story problem/resolution graphic organizer and have the students complete it about a familiar story of their choice. They could even use their favorite movie or TV show in completing it. Have them share with a friend.
- Provide a station for students to read a book at their independent reading level and then complete the plot/story problem/resolution graphic organizer.
- Ask the students change the characters in a story. Have them share in their response journals how it might change the problem, events, and/or resolution.
- Ask the students to rewrite a story changing the problem, events, and resolution.
- Ask the students to recall a problem they have encountered. Have them write it as a story including the problem, events, and resolution.

Plot/Story Problem/Resolution
Across the Curriculum

Math	• Teachers may refer to problem and resolutions when students are working on story problems. They are presented with the problem and must find the resolution.

Science	• Science experiments
	   ○ The "question" is the problem
	   ○ The "conclusion" is the resolution
	• Inventors were successful because they had a "problem" they wanted to resolve.

Social Studies	• Famous people who are known for solving a problem they had:
	   ○ Helen Keller
	   ○ Martin L. King, Jr.
	   ○ Abraham Lincoln

Other	• Art: Finding the problem in an art print
Comments	• Use the terms plot, problem and resolution when discussing situations that happen in the classroom when talking to students.

Order of Important Events

Order of Important Events, Sequence

Teacher Talk

What: (What is the Order of Important Events and Sequence?) Most stories have a sequence of events, which are organized in the order in which they happen. Sometimes the author uses time words, such as: first, next, before, after that, finally, at last, etc. to signal the order of the events.

Why: (Why does it help you as a reader?) To understand a story the reader must understand the sequence of events in the story. Some informative texts, such as a How To story, include a sequence of events that must be followed carefully.

When: (When is it used during reading?) The sequence is used to understand when and why something happens in a story. Directions for doing something require the exact use of a sequence of activities.

What does research tell us about this strategy?

Beck, McCaslin, and McKeown (1981) state in their research article on setting the purpose for reading , "The sequence of events as part of a story promotes comprehension."

Beck, I.L. & McCaslin, E.S., & McKeown, M.G. (1981). **Basal readers' purpose for story reading: Smoothly paving the road or setting up a detour?** The Elementary School Journal, *81*(3). P.156-161.

What is expected at this level?

Students beginning in kindergarten can sequence events in drama and listening. As reading skills develop the strategy is moved into reading and writing.

What prior knowledge or schema do the students need to have?
Students must have an understanding of time order. Actions happen in an order.

What are the cautions and tips when teaching this strategy?

• To be successful, students often need to be able to follow directions in the order they are given.

• Students should understand clue words such as first, next, then, last, finally, etc.

Expectations

Order of Important Events, Sequence			
Grade Introduced – I Grade Developed – D	K	1	2
Reading	I	D	D
Writing			

Order of Important Events, Sequence

Introduction

Activity 1

Materials: Order of Important Events/Sequence Definition Chart
Order of Event Pictures Cards(PDR-CD)

- Prepare and display the Order of Important Events/Sequence Definition Chart shown below. A blackline master is also provided on the PDR-CD. The teacher should enlarge the chart, create their own example of the chart, or make a transparency to show the students.

- Use the definition chart to introduce the strategy. Name and define the strategy, including why and when to use the strategy during reading. (Refer to Teacher Talk)

Order of Important Events, Sequence

The events in the story happen in order.
Retell the story and use time words such as first, next, before, then, after, that, finally,

Key Phrases
- The orders of events are first_____, next _____, then _____, last_____ etc.
- The pictures I have in my mind are _____.

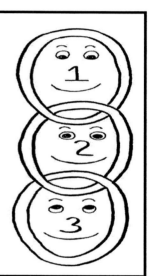

- When discussing the definition and key phrases use an example of a situation or familiar book to activate prior knowledge.

- Display and review the Definition Chart. Think aloud and explain the definition to the students.

Model

Activity 1

Materials: Order of Important Events, Sequence Definition Chart
Picture book **Goldilocks and the Three Bears**

- Review the Order of Important Definition Chart with the students.

- Select 3-5 pictures from the picture book <u>Goldilocks and the Three Bears</u> to think aloud about the order of the events.

- ***Today, I am going to use pictures of the story <u>Goldilocks and the Three Bears</u> and I am going to talk about the order the way the story happened.***

- Think aloud as you share with the students.

- *I don't think Goldilocks could sit in the chair before she went in the house of the three bears Goldilocks would not have gone in the house if the bears had not left for their walk.*

- Select 2 more familiar books and model why the order of events were important to the story.

- *I am now thinking about a story we read in class. I am thinking of _____.* **Think aloud** with the students and model why the sequence of the events was important to the story.

- *After thinking about these stories, I realize the order of events in a story is important.*

- *Now it is your turn. I am going to display another familiar book and the picture of the events.*

- *This time turn to your partner and say,*

  The important events are first____, next ____, then ____, finally____ etc.

- Allow students enough time to share their thinking with their partner. Ask several students to share their thinking.

Guided Practice

Activity 1

Materials: Order of Important Events/Sequence Definition Chart
Copy of <u>A Weekend at Grandma's</u> (PDR-CD)
Highlighter

- Review the Order of Important Events / Sequence using the definition chart.

- *Today, I am going to read a story and think about the order of the events. I want to know if the order when things happen is important.*

- Display the story, <u>A Weekend at Grandma's</u>, read the story aloud to the students. A blackline master is provided that can be made into a transparency or enlarged for the students to see.

- Refer to the definition chart and use the key words: first, next, before, after, and finally to demonstrate how they can be used to retell a story.

- Reread the story and talk about the key words used to organize the order of events. Use a high lighter to highlight key words.

- *I know the order of events were important in this story. When I think of how I do things, order is important. I need to put my shoes on before I tie them. I need to put toothpaste on my toothbrush before I brush my teeth. I use key words to help me sequence events as I read and write.*

- Ask the students to stop to talk. Ask them to retell what they did this morning when they got up before coming to school. *Turn to your partner and say, The order of events were first ____, next ____, then____, last ____, etc.*

- Repeat the above procedure on other days using stories that you have read to the children, shared reading texts, and guided reading.

Activity 2

> Materials: Order of Important Events/Sequence Definition Chart
> Graphic Organizer for Order of Important Events (PDR-CD)
> Text used in shared reading

- Review the Order of Important Events / Sequence Definition Chart.
- ***Today as we read a story, I want you to think about events in the order in which they happen.***
- Read the story with the students. Think aloud stopping to discuss the order of events as you read using key phrases and order words.
- ***I know that the order of events in a story is very important.***
- Display a chart or transparency of the graphic organizer that is provided at the end of the lesson for Order of Important Events for students. ***I can use a graphic organizer to help me place the events in the order they happened. The key words will help me to organize the events.***
- **Think aloud** as you complete the graphic organizer.
- ***I think using a graphic organizer is very helpful in sequencing the events of a story.***
- Ask students to stop to talk about the order of events. Allow students to share how a graphic organizer helped in sequencing the events.

Shared Reading

> Materials: Teacher selected text
> Order of Important Events Graphic Organizer (PDR-CD)

- Read the story with the students.
- Have students stop to talk. ***Turn to your partner and say, The order of events were first _____, next _____, then_____, last _____, etc.***

Options: 1. Teacher and students complete the Order of Important Events Graphic Organizer together. 2. Make picture cards of the important events and the students work with their partner to put them in order. 3. Students use their student response journal to draw the events in order.

Small Group Reading

> Materials: Texts used in small group reading
> Index Cards

- Ask students to reread their text from small reading group or guided reading.
- Give students four index cards and have them draw four pictures showing four events from the story (one on each card).
- Students then write a sentence on each card about the event.
- Have students place the cards in the same sequence as they happened in the story.

- The students can staple the cards in order with a blank index card on top, write the title of the story, and retold by _____ on the top card to make a cover.
- Then, the students share their retellings with one another and discuss the order of events.

Option: 1. After reading the guided reading book the first time, the teacher retells the story using the key terms for students as they listen. 2. Ask students to turn to their partner and retell the story using key terms and key phrases. 3. Use this activity in a station. Provide familiar books and ask students to reread and retell the story on index cards.

Independent Reading

Activity 1

Materials: Texts on independent reading levels
Order of Important Events Graphic Organizer (PDR-CD)

- Student reads a book at their independent reading level.
- After reading, the students complete the Order of Important Events Graphic Organizer.
- Allow time for the students to share.

Activity 2

Materials: Index Cards

- The student draws or writes a short story on index cards.
- Each card will tell about an event in their story.
- The students work with their partner and trade story cards.
- Each student reads their partners cards and places them in the order that the events happen.
- The student checks the partner to make sure the cards are in the correct order.
- Students discuss any changes that need to be made and read the story together.

A Step Beyond

- Student draws pictures to tell a story. The student then writes sentences to tell the story. The student sits in the author's chair and reads the story. After listening to the story, the students turn to their partners and retell the story using the key words (first, next, before, after, etc.).
- Students draw pictures and/or write about their (day, afternoons, vacation, weekend, how to do something together, etc.) The events must be sequenced correctly.
- Provide cut up comic strips or pictures from a wordless books in envelopes.

Number the envelopes and the frames of the comics. Begin with wordless frames. The children sequence the frames. Those who are writing can write a few sentences about the frames using the key words.

- Use science materials for children to sequence and demonstrate the steps in a science experiment.

- Parents can be interviewed about something special that they do. The child draws pictures and/or writes about the thing his parent does (making toast, working a puzzle, setting the table, mowing the lawn, etc.)

- A child can demonstrate how to do something like blowing bubbles, sharpening a pencil, or brushing their teeth. He/she uses the key words on the steps of the process before they model it.

- Make copies of a small text with one or two lines on each page. Remove the page numbers. The students sequence the pictures and write the text on the pages.

Order of Important Events
Across the Curriculum

Math	• Many times when solving a math problem one operation must be performed before the next.
Science	• Science experiment (has a certain order).
Social Studies	• Order of historical events
Other	• Parts of a song are in order to tell a story. • Need to follow directions in a given order to complete an art project. • Use of computers and ways to get to a certain problem.

Summary

Summary

Teacher Talk

What: (What is a summary?) A summary is a short paragraph retelling of the most important ideas and details in the text. The retelling is done in sequence, including the beginning, middle, and end.

Why: (Why does it help you as a reader?) Summarizing helps the reader understand the most important information given by the author.

When: (When do you use it during reading?) The reader uses summarization when retelling only the important parts of the text.

What does research tell us about this strategy?

In the book *Teaching Reading in the 21st Century*, leading reading researchers tell us, "Most text contains much more information than a reader can focus on and learn; consequently, determining what is important is a crucial and frequently required strategy."

Graves, M.F., & Juel, C., & Graves, B.B. (1998). *Teaching reading in the 21st century*. Boston: Allyn and Bacon Publishing.

What is expected of the students when using this strategy?

Students are expected to retell a spoken or written message by summarizing.

What prior knowledge or schema do the students need to know?

In summarizing, students are collecting the most important ideas to use in a short retelling. The concept of main idea and supporting details should be taught before the summarization. Students need to understand sequence of events to retell the events in the correct order.

What are the cautions and tips when teaching this strategy?

- Students need an understanding of main idea and supporting details.

- Begin teaching children to summarize by thinking about the beginning, middle, and end of the story. It is difficult for some students to understand the difference between a summary and retelling.

- Model for the students by summarizing what you did during a certain period of the day. Use key words and phrases as you model and state what you did and some of the important things about the activity. Be sure you use the word "summary" or "summarize" when you are modeling. Students at the K-2 level need to hear the strategy name and see it modeled as often as possible.

Expectations

Summary			
Grade Introduced – I **Grade Developed - D**	**K**	**1**	**2**
Reading	I	D	D
Writing			I

Summary

Introduction

Materials: Summary Definition Chart

- Prepare and display the Summary Definition Chart shown below. A blackline master is also provided at the end of the unit. The teacher should enlarge the chart, create their own example of the chart, or make a transparency to show the students.

- Use the definition chart to introduce the strategy. Name and define the strategy, including why and when to use the strategy during reading. (Refer to Teacher Talk)

Summary

To summarize retell the important ideas in sequence.   Tell details from the beginning, middle and end

Key Phrases   Beginning   Middle   End
- A summary of the story is_____.

- When discussing the definition and key phrases use an example of a situation or familiar book to activate prior knowledge.
- Display and review the Definition Chart.
- Think aloud and explain the definition to the students.

Model

Activity 1

Materials: Summary Definition Chart
3-4 Familiar texts
Chart paper

- ***Sometimes I need to tell someone how to do something but may not have a lot of time to explain every little detail. I need to tell them in a shorter way. I include the important details but don't take the time to include everything. When I do this, I am giving them a summary of how to do it.***

- *** I can also do this with stories. I can give a summary of the story by telling only the important details in the story.***

- Review the summary definition chart and display the book you have chosen to use.

- ***I wonder if I could give a summary of _____. I think I will give it a try. I know a story has a beginning, middle, and end.***

- Use think aloud to model this process. As you come up with a sentence for the beginning of the story, write it on the chart paper. Read the sentence aloud.

- *I think this is a summary of the beginning of the story because it retells the beginning of the story in a short way.*
- Follow this same process to model the middle and ending of the story.
- *Now I am going to read all of my sentences and see if it is a summary or short retelling of the story.*
- Read the sentences aloud. *This is my summary for _____.*
- Repeat using 2 more familiar texts.
- The last familiar text. The students give it a try.
- *This time I want you to stop to talk and summarize the story_____. Turn to your partner and say, The beginning _____ ,the middle _____and the end _____. The summary of the story is _____.*
- Allow students enough time to share their thinking with their partner. Ask several students to share their thinking and discuss.

Option: For added support use the following steps.

- Divide the sheet of chart paper into 3 sections.
- Label the first section *Beginning,* the second section *Middle,* and the last section *Ending.*
- Read the book aloud to the students.
- Use think aloud talk to model the process of writing a summary of the story. Use the same process you used in Activity 1. Instead of writing on the board, write the beginning, middle, and ending sentences under the appropriate heading on the chart paper.
- Go back and reread each of the sentences. Explain that they are a short retelling or summary of the story.

Guided Practice

       Materials: Picture book
                  Student response journals

- Review the Summary Definition chart.
- *Today I am going to read _____ and then we are going to write a summary of the story.*
- Read the story aloud to the students.
- *Let's think about our story and talk about the beginning. Turn to your partner and say, The beginning of the story is about _____.*
- Allow students just enough time to talk about the beginning of the story. Allow a few students to share their responses.
- *Now, let's think about what happened in the middle of the story. Turn to your*

partner and say, The middle of the story is about _____.

- Allow students just enough time to talk about the middle of the story. Allow a few students to share their responses.
- *Finally, let's talk about what happened at the end of the story. Turn to your partner and say, The end of the story is about _____.*
- Allow students enough time to share their thinking with their partner. Ask several students to share their thinking and discuss.

Note: If their responses are more of a retelling of the entire story, guide them in sharing only the most important ideas. It may be necessary to write more than one sentence. Let them know that is all right as long as they are sharing only the important details. Write their final responses on the board. Follow this same process for the middle and end of the story. Read the sentences from the board with students. Ask them if the sentences are a summary of the story. How do they know?

Read Aloud – Multiple Strategy Practice
Materials: New Picture books for Read Aloud
3-4 Introduced strategies for practice

- As new strategies are introduced it is important to continue to practice previously introduced strategies and orchestrate them with the new strategy. Choose 3-4 strategies that have been introduced in previous lessons to review and practice with the new strategy.
- Set up the read aloud by selecting appropriate places to stop in the text to practice the strategies selected. Prepare a sticky note for each strategy writing a key phrase for the strategy to be practiced. The sticky notes are placed on the page as a signal as you read to stop and ask the students to turn to their partner and practice the strategy. Example: *Turn to your partner and say, I predict …and tell you partner what you predict and why.*
- Allow students enough time to share their thinking with their partner. Ask several students to share their thinking and discuss.
- Continue to read until you come to the next stopping point. Repeat practicing another selected strategy.

Note: Select texts that support the strategies for practice. Example strategies practiced could be; predicting, asking a question, describe a character, setting, and summary.

Independent Practice
The students have had several experiences with main idea and supporting details during oral reading and whole group. Independent practice may be given during shared reading, small group reading, and independent reading.

Materials: Big book
Summary Graphic Organizer (PDR-CD)

- Read the book aloud to the students.
- Show the students the Summary Graphic Organizer provided at the end of the lesson. Explain that the organizer has the same sections on it as what you have been modeling for writing a summary.
- Have the students complete the Summary Graphic Organizer for the story they just heard. As the students complete their organizer, have them share it with you or a partner.

Small Group Reading/Independent Reading

Activity 1
Materials: Texts for small group reading
                   Reading response journal or Summary Graphic Organizer

- After the small group or guided reading lesson ask students to draw or write a summary including the beginning, middle, and end. Be sure to include the important ideas and details.
- Ask students to stop to talk to their partner to share their summaries.
- Allow several students to share their summary.

Activity 2
Materials: Texts on independent levels that provide a summary of the story on the book flap or back cover

- Share with the students that some books give you a summary of what the book is about. The summary will help you know if you want to read the book.
- The teacher or students read book summaries and tell whether they would like to read the book and why or why not.

A Step Beyond

- Provide a station with books at the independent level of the students. They read the book and draw or write a summary in their response journal or on the Summary Graphic Organizer.
- Students think of their favorite movie. Explain that movie previews are a summary of the movie. They write a summary of their favorite movie for a friend.
- Ask the students to write a summary of their day for Mom and Dad. Tell them to be sure it is a summary and not a retelling.
- Ask the students to design a cover for their favorite book. The front should have a title and picture. They can fold their paper so it has a flap to write a summary of the book or they may write the summary of the book on the back.

Summary
Across the Curriculum

Math	• Summarize how they solved a problem
Science	• Science experiments • Reports • Science text selections
Social Studies	• Reports • Social Studies text selections
Other	• Writing: Write a summary of an activity or event such as a field trip. • Write a summary of their day at school. • Write a summary about getting ready for lunch or to go home.

Comprehension

Text to Support Meaning

Text to Support Meaning

Teacher Talk

What: (What is Text to Support Meaning?): The supporting details are small bits of information that help define and give more information about the main idea. They tell who, what, where, when, why and how. These details are stated directly in the text. Good readers pay attention to these details and use them to support or give evidence for their thinking.

Why: (Why does it help you as a reader?): Good readers use these details to help them prove their thinking.

When: (When is it used during reading?) When a question needs to be answered to confirm thinking, or when meaning breaks down as the child reads.

What does research tell us about this strategy?
"The ability to find needed information documents the reader's understanding"
– Frank Smith (1994)

What is expected at this level when using the strategy?
The students monitor their own comprehension and search for clues in the text to support the meaning. They can identify supporting details or ask questions they have as they participate in read alouds, shared reading, small group reading and independent reading.

What prior knowledge or schema do the students need to have?
The student must know how to search the text for the answer to the question. They anticipate meaning and work to make sense of the texts.

What are the cautions and tips when teaching this strategy?

- The text must be an appropriate reading level to enable students to search the text for information to support their thinking.

- Task may need to be modified according to ability level of the students.

Expectations

Text To Support Meaning			
Grade Introduced – I **Grade Developed - D**	**K**	**1**	**2**
Reading	I	D	D
Writing		I	D

Text to Support Meaning

Introduction

> Materials: Text to Support Meaning Definition Chart

- Prepare and display the Main Idea and Supporting Details Definition Chart shown below. A blackline master is also provided on PDR-CD. The teacher should enlarge the chart, create their own example of the chart, or make a transparency to show the students.

- Use the definition chart to introduce the strategy. Name and define the strategy, including why and when to use the strategy during reading. (Refer to Teacher Talk)

Text to Support Meaning

Good readers use details to prove (tell or show) their thinking.
The details tell who, what, where, when, why and how about the main idea.

Key Phrases
- This part of the story shows …
- This part of the story tells …
- This part tells …

- When discussing the definition and key phrases use an example of a situation or familiar book to activate prior knowledge about the strategy prediction.

Model

> Materials: Text to Support Meaning Definition Chart
> Text to Support Meaning Selection/Jill's Birthday Surprise
> Chart of Jill's Birthday Surprise (PDR-CD)

- Review the Text to Support Meaning Definition Chart with the students.

- Prepare and display a chart or transparency of Jill's Birthday Surprise that is provided at the end of the lesson.

- ***Today I am going to read a story. The name of the story is Jill's Birthday Surprise. Sometimes, after I read the title of a story, I have several questions.***

  - *I wonder who is in the story. Is it just Jill?*
  - *I wonder what the surprise will be.*
  - *I wonder when it happens. When is Jill's birthday?*
  - *I wonder where Jill is when she gets the surprise.*
  - *I wonder how Jill is feeling and why.*

- Hold up your hand. Quickly review using your hand for the supporting details.

  When I am reading, I can use my fingers to help me   remember that a story often includes the who, what, when, where, and why. These are called the supporting details.

- *Those details can help you answer the questions you had about the story and understand what it is about.*
- *As I read the story, I am going to see if some of my questions are answered in the text.*
- Read the story aloud to the students.
- Think aloud about your questions. Go back and find in the text where the answers to were. Use a high lighter to highlight the parts of the text that answered your questions.
- *I now know that text does support the meaning of the story. The text gives me more details and makes it possible for me to prove the answers to questions I may have when I read.*
- *Now it's your turn to give it a try.* **Ask the students to stop to talk about other words in the text that give them more information about Jill and her birthday.**

    Turn to your partner and say: This part of the story tells _____ .
- Allow students enough time to share their thinking with their partner. Ask several students to share their evidence and discuss.

Guided Practice
      Materials: Text to Support Meaning Definition Chart
                   Big Book - Teacher selected text

- Review the Text to Support Meaning Definition Chart with the students.
- Hold up your hand. **Today as we read I want you to listen for the who, what, when, where, and why in the story.**
- Introduce and read the book. **Think aloud** and guide the students in answering who, what, when, where, and why. Ask the students to provide evidence for their responses. As each response is discussed, have the students come and locate the text that gave them their information.
- *Today you used the text to support the meaning of the story we read. You were able to provide evidence for your answers. That is what a good reader does.*

Shared Reading
      Materials: Big Book

- Review the definition with the students.
- Introduce the big book you will share together. During the reading of the book, stop and ask questions about the story. The students may use a pointer to "prove" their answer by pointing in the text where they found the supporting detail.

Small Group Reading
      Materials: Texts used in small group

- Students reread the book used in small reading group.

- When they are finished, ask questions about the story.
- The students must find the answers in the text and share with their partner
- Allow students to share with the group.

Read Aloud – Multiple Strategy Practice
Materials: New Picture Books for Read Aloud
                     3-5 Introduced strategies for practice

- As new strategies are introduced it is important to continue to practice previously introduced strategies and orchestrate them with the new strategy. Choose 3-4 strategies that have been introduced in previous lessons to review and practice with the new strategy.

- Set up the read aloud by selecting appropriate places to stop in the text to practice the strategies selected. Prepare a sticky note for each strategy writing a key phrase for the strategy to be practiced. The sticky notes are placed on the page as a signal as you read to stop and ask the students to turn to their partner and practice the strategy. Example: ***Turn to your partner and say, I predict …and tell you partner what you predict and why.***

- Allow students enough time to share their thinking with their partner. Ask several students to share their thinking and discuss.

- Continue to read until you come to the next stopping point. Repeat practicing another selected strategy.

Note: Select texts that support the strategies for practice. Example strategies practiced could be; predicting, asking a question, describe a character, setting, and summary. Ask students to provide evidence for their thinking.

Independent Reading
Materials: Texts on independent reading levels
                     Text Supporting Meaning Graphic Organizer (PDR-CD)

- Students select and read a book on their independent reading level.

- Students who are ready to write about their story can complete the Text Supporting Meaning Graphic Organizer using the text they read. These students share their findings with a partner. The teacher may need to model for some students the process of completing the graphic organizer before they do it on their own.

A Step Beyond

- Students may share information about a story with a partner. They then show in the text where they found the information.

- Students pair with another student that reads on the same independent reading level. They read a book of their choice. Each student then writes questions about their story. When both have completed their questions, they switch papers.

- They read the story their partner just read and answer the questions. They may write down the page number of the book where they found the answer.

Note: When first beginning this activity, you may want to reduce the number of supporting details the student will search and share. A lower level reader might search for the who and what, initially. Then the others could be added subsequently.

Text to Support Meaning
Across the Curriculum

Math	• **Reading a story problem** • **Explaining their reasoning behind their answer** • **Weeding out unnecessary information in a story problem**
Science **Social Studies**	• **Finding proof for answers when using science and social studies texts**
Other	• **Following examples**

Inferences
Predictions
Drawing Conclusions

Inferences: Predictions / Drawing Conclusions

Teacher Talk

What: (What are inferences, predictions and drawing conclusions?)

When reading, use information from the text (story details) and what you know (life experiences) to make inferences. That means you go beyond the author's words to understand what is not said in the text. When you make inferences, you make predictions and draw conclusions. To do this you think of logical outcomes (now or in the future). It is always important to give evidence or tell what information in the text helped you.

Inference is the umbrella strategy and includes predictions and drawing conclusions. When making an inference take information from the text and what you know to figure out something that is not stated in the text. This includes:

- **Prediction** is making a smart guess or hypothesis about what may happen in the future.

- **Drawing Conclusions** is when the reader takes information from the text and comes to a new understanding.

Why: (Why does it help you as a reader?) Readers use predictions to form a hypothesis of what may happen. This keeps readers engaged in the text using prior knowledge to compare and combine with new knowledge creating a new understanding or questioning the author. Using prior knowledge to make predictions and draw conclusions helps readers stay engaged and active in the reading process enhancing understanding and memory of the text.

When: (When is it used during reading?) Readers make, confirm, and adjust their predictions before, during and after reading. When reading readers draw conclusion they use prior knowledge and what they have learned from the text to construct new knowledge.

What does research tell us about this strategy?

Research by Hall (1990) states, "Inferring allows readers to make their own discoveries with out the direct comment of the author."

"Proficient readers infer implicit notions from the text and create meaning based on those notions. If readers don't infer, they will not grasp the deeper essence of texts they read."

Harvey, S. & Goudvis, A. (2000). Strategies That Work: Teaching Comprehension to Enhance Understanding. York, ME: Stenhouse

What is expected at this level when using the strategy?

Students at this level make predictions before reading to set a purpose for reading. They use schema to predict meaning, events, outcomes and makes sense of the text. Students draw conclusions from information given in the text and give evidence for their interpretations and conclusions.

What prior knowledge or schema do the students need to have?

- Students need a concept of next or what comes after before they can make predictions.

- Readers use the information in the text and their schema to wonder and question about the missing information. They infer, predict, or draw a conclusion as they look ahead thinking about how situations and events unfold.

What are cautions and tips when teaching this strategy?

- Making predictions and drawing conclusions is more successful for students when using stories, concepts and subjects they are familiar with allowing them to use their prior knowledge. Begin with pictures and stories that are familiar and scaffold to new subjects.

- Model for students how to examine pictures and texts looking for clues and information to generate predictions and conclusions. Many times students need to be reminded and encouraged to think before making inferences.

- Students will make some predictions that do not really happen in the text. They may become discouraged. It is very important that they understand that their predictions are acceptable if they can provide information from the text to substantiate their prediction or conclusion.

- When selecting a text for inferences, use a new text that provides multiple opportunities to making predictions and/or drawing conclusions. A familiar text provides a clear example of how we make predictions and draw conclusions for those students who need reteaching.

- Model and practice with different types of texts.

Expectations

Inferences: Predictions			
Grade Introduced – I Grade Developed – D	K	1	2
Reading	I	D	D
Writing			

Inferences: Drawing Conclusions			
Grade Introduced – I Grade Developed – D	K	1	2
Reading		I	D
Writing			

Inferences: Predictions, Drawing Conclusions

Introduction

Materials: Predictions and Drawing Conclusions Definition Chart

- Prepare and display the Inferences, Predictions, and Drawing Conclusions Definition Chart like the one shown below. A blackline master is also provided on PDR-CD. The teacher should enlarge the chart, create their own example of the chart, or make a transparency to show the students.

- Use the definition chart to introduce the strategy. Name and define the strategy, including why and when to use the strategy during reading. (Refer to Teacher Talk)

Predict

Predict or "make a guess" about what will happen. Tell why you predict that.

Key Phrase:
- I predict _____ because _____.
- My prediction was right because _____.
- I am changing my prediction because_____.

Model

Activity 1

Materials: Predictions and Drawing Conclusion Definition Chart
4-5 Pictures for making predictions

- Display and review the definition with the students.

- *You make inferences when you take information and what you know to figure something out. I am going to make some inferences today using pictures.*

- *I will use the information from the picture along with what I know and make some inferences.*

- Display one of the pictures you selected. Think aloud to model the strategy using the pre-selected picture.

Example: A picture of a birthday party.

- *Looking at this picture, I think the children are at a birthday party. I think this because there are balloons hanging from the ceiling and presents on the table. I think the birthday child is the girl wearing red because she is holding a present in her hand. I think she is getting ready to open her presents. I also think the little girl is turning seven years old. I drew this conclusion because she had seven candles on her cake and I know the number of candles on a birthday cake stand for the number of years old the one having the birthday is.*

- Display a picture that you have selected that provides opportunities to make predictions.
- *Now I want you to give it a try. I am going to hold up a new picture. Take a few seconds to study the picture.*
- *Repeat this process with two more pictures to model for the students.*
- Ask the students look at the picture and think about what is going on in the picture and what they know about what is going to make a prediction.
- *Now I want you to turn and talk to your partner and say, I think _____. I think this because _____.*
- Allow students enough time to share their thinking with their partner. Ask several students to share their thinking and provide evidence.

Activity 2
     Materials: Predictions and Drawing Conclusion Definition Chart
                      Picture book with 4-5 clear opportunities to model predictions
- Display the definition chart and review it with the students.
- *Today during our read aloud I am going to show you how I think about the text and make predictions as I read. I will use things I know and the words in the text to think about what will happen next.*
- Read the book aloud to the students. Stop at pre-selected points and use key phrases to think aloud about what you predict will happen next. Tell the students what information from the text helped you make your prediction.
- Save the last stopping point for making a prediction at the end of the book for students to give it a try.
- Ask the students stop to talk and make predictions.
- *Now I want you to give it a try. Turn to your partner and say; I think _____. I think this because _____.*
- Allow students enough time to share their thinking with their partner. Allow several students to share their thinking and provide evidence from the text.
- Finish the story. Discuss with the students that it is ok if their prediction was not the same as the author's. They just chose to end the story differently.

Note: Students may predict different outcomes in the story, remind students that their predictions may be different, but they must be able to tell what information in the text lead them to make that prediction.

Guided Practice

Shared Reading
     Materials: Predictions and Drawing Conclusions Definition Chart
                      Big book (New) selected by teacher providing multiple opportunities to make predictions

- Display the definition chart and review it with the student.
- ***Looking at the cover, what do you think the story will be about? Why? Today as I read I am going to ask you to practice making prediction with your partner as we read the story.***
- Read and stop at pre-selected points using key phrases to ask the students to turn to their partners, make predictions, and give evidence for their thinking.
- Allow students enough time to share their thinking with their partner. Allow several students to share their thinking and discuss how it helped them to understand the story better.
- ***You made some good predictions as we read the story. Can we draw a conclusion from our story? Are we able to take what we learned and come up with a new understanding that was not stated in the story?***

Option: 1. Students draw or write their prediction to the end of the story and come back later to share. 2. Students draw or write a new ending to the story using predictions made during stop to talk. 3. The teacher and students work together to make a list of the predictions made during the story and discuss if they are reasonable predictions or not. Could that happen and why?

Independent Practice

Activity 1

Small group reading

> Materials: Predictions and Drawing Conclusions Definition Chart
> New texts for small group reading

- Display and review the Inference Definition Chart.
- Before reading the new text with the students, have them look through the book and use pictures to make predictions about the story. Ask students to share why they made that prediction.
- After reading the story, have students share which of their predictions were the same as the author's. Have the students draw a conclusion from the story.

Activity 2

> Materials: Predictions and Drawing Conclusions Definition Chart
> Various texts on independent reading levels

- Ask students' to work with a partner at their independent reading levels.
- They will read the same book together. As the students read, have them stop and make predictions about what they think will happen next in the story.
- When they are finished reading, have them share the conclusions they drew from the story. Students may write their conclusions in their student response journals or draw a picture about their thinking.

A Step Beyond

- Share only part of a story. Have the students use their prediction skills to write an ending to the story. They can use the author's chair to read their story endings aloud to the class.

- Share pictures of things that are familiar to the students. The students write or draw what they think will happen in the next picture of the story.

- Students write a riddle and ask others to predict what will happen next. Example: "I am at the beach with my grandmother. We have a bucket. Grandmother wants some new shells for her collection. What do you think we are going to do?"

- Riddles could be shared at a station. The students read a riddle and write what they think will happen next, and illustrate it.

- The riddles could be used as a bulletin board: What Will Happen Next?

- Students have a day called "Prediction Day". Make predictions throughout the day and provide evidence for thinking.

- Students decide how a character feels when listening, reading or viewing pictures. For example, if a character is crying, predict why the character might be feeling? The teacher models actions that represent emotion, such as stomping feet or frowning. The students predict which emotion is being modeled. Then students could try new actions with a partner or draw pictures of emotions. Authors many times "show" or describe how a character feels without directly saying the feeling word.

Cause and Effect
(Literal and Inferential)

Cause and Effect

Teacher Talk

What: (What is Cause and Effect?) Cause and Effect is defined below at two levels, literal and inferred.

Literal: When you think about a cause and effect, you think about two things:

> What happens or the result (effect)

> Why it happens (cause)

Sometimes the author gives us both the cause and the effect in the text. The author may use words to show this relationship such as: because, as a result, therefore, since, so, etc.

Example: Mary ate too much candy at the movies (cause), so she
had a stomach ache that night. (effect)

Inferred: Sometimes the author may not give us the cause or effect in the text.

If you are given the cause, use your prior knowledge about people, places, and events to predict what will probably happen in the future. If you are given the effect, ask why something happened.

Example: Prior Knowledge: I know if you stay up late you will be sleepy the next day.

Text: Jim stayed up past midnight with his friends.

Inferred: Jim and his friends are sleepy.

Why: (Why does it help you as a reader?) Identifying the cause and effect helps the reader make connections with characters and the story plot.

When: (When is it used during reading?) You use this strategy to determine <u>what</u> and <u>why</u> something happens in the story.

What does research tell us about this strategy?

What is expected at this level when using the strategy?

In kindergarten it will be mostly literal. As they mature, you then begin to model and practice inferred cause and effect.

What prior knowledge or schema do the students need to have? Pam

Students must have prior knowledge of the experience or concept in order to connect the <u>what</u> and <u>why</u> of cause and effect.

What are the cautions and tips when teaching this strategy?

- The text should be read aloud or at reading levels appropriate for the children.
- The use of a graphic organizer can assist in making this task easier for some students.
- Some students may confuse the cause with the effect.
  Use mini lessons to further model and provide guided practice.
- Students must use prior knowledge and experiences to connect to the "what" and "why" of cause and effect.

Expectations

Cause and Effect - Literal			
Grade Introduced – I **Grade Developed – D**	**K**	**1**	**2**
Reading	I	D	D
Writing			

Cause and Effect

Introduction

Materials: Cause and Effect Definition Chart

- Prepare and display the Cause and Effect Definition chart like the one shown below. A blackline master is also provided at the end of the lesson. The teacher should enlarge the chart, create their own example of the chart, or make a transparency to show the students.

- Use the definition chart to introduce the strategy. Name and define the strategy, including why and when to use the strategy during reading. (Refer to Teacher Talk)

- When discussing the definition and key phrases use an example of a situation or familiar book to activate prior knowledge about the strategy prediction.

Cause and Effect

Cause
Why it happens

Effect
What happens

Key Phrases
- _____ because _____.

Model

Materials: Cause and Effect Definition Chart
Cause and Effect Pictures (PDR-CD)

- Display and review the Cause and Effect definition chart.

- *I know from the definition that if I recognize the cause and effect it helps me to understand what happened. Today I am going to use some pictures of cause and effect to see if they help me understand what is happening.*

- Share one pair of the cause and effect pictures.

- *Let me think for a minute. I know that the effect is what happens. I also know the cause is why it happened. I think this picture is the effect because_____ __. I think this picture is the cause because _____. This helps me to understand why_____.*

- Share another pair of pictures and use think aloud talk to model in the same way.

- *Now I want you to give it a try.* Put a pair of pictures for all to see.

- *Stop to talk about which picture is the effect and which is the cause Tell why you think the way you do.*

Guided Practice

Activity 1

      Materials: Cause and Effect Definition Chart

                     Cause and Effect (Literal) sentences transparency or chart

- Review the definition chart.
- Display transparency or chart of the Cause and Effect (literal) sentences that are provided below.
- *We have practiced cause and effect with pictures. Today we are going to practice finding the cause and effect with words.*
- *Sometimes the author uses words that tell us the cause and effect in the story. Let's practice finding the cause and effect in each sentence.*
- Cover up everything except for the sentences you are using. Read the sentences aloud with the students. **I think I will underline the cause and circle the effect.**
- **Ted put up his umbrella because it was raining outside.**
- **I know the effect is Ted put his umbrella. That is what happened.** Circle the effect. **I know the cause is because it was raining outside. That is why he put his umbrella up.** Underline the cause.
- **Now I want you to do some. I will show you a sentence. Stop to talk about the cause and effect. Then we will underline the cause and circle the effect together.**
- Practice one sentence at a time. This will allow the students to think about each one and then check themselves as the teacher circles the effect and underlines the cause.
- **Today we practiced finding the literal cause and effect in sentences. Knowing the cause and effect helps us better understand what is happening.**

Activity 2

      Materials: Cause and Effect Definition Chart

                     Teacher selected text for modeling

- Review cause and effect using the definition chart.
- *We have practiced finding cause and effect with pictures and in sentences. Today we will practice finding the cause and effect in a story.*
- Introduce the story you plan to read.
- *Listen closely as I read the story to you. There may be more than one example of cause and effect. Let's read and see.*
- Read the story to the students. As you are reading, ask the students to find the examples of cause and effect and share.
- *Today we found examples of cause and effect in our story. I want you to stop to talk about how knowing cause and effect helped you better understand the story.*

Independent Practice

Shared Reading

Materials: Teacher selected text

- As the students are participating in shared reading, have them find examples of cause and effect.

Small Group Reading

Materials: Text used in small group

- As the students are reading during small reading groups, ask them identify examples of cause and effect.

Option: Students work in pairs and each finding either the cause or the effect.

Independent Reading

Materials: Various texts at independent reading levels
Student response journals

- Students read a book on their independent reading level.
- Ask students to find examples of cause and effect in their story.
- Ask students to write the cause and effect in their student response journal.

Model - Cause and Effect Inferred

Materials: Cause and Effect Definition Chart

- Review the definition chart with the students.
- *You have learned to find literal cause and effect. That is when the author tells you the cause and effect through their words.*
- *Today I am going to try to find inferred cause and effect. The author may tell me the cause but not the effect. Or the author may give me the effect but not the cause. I think I will give it a try.*
- Write this sentence on the board:

  Jim put up his umbrella when he walked out the door.

- *In this sentence I know what Jim is doing. The author gave me the effect. The author does not give me the cause. I know people use umbrellas when it is raining. I think the cause is that it is raining outside. I will try another.*
- Write this sentence on the board:

  Jessica was excited when she did well on her spelling test.

- *In this sentence I know Jessica did well on her spelling test. That is the effect. I know that to do well on a spelling test, it is important to study. I think the cause or the reason Jessica did well on her test is because she practiced spelling the words before the test.*

- *I am going to show you a sentence with an inferred cause.*
- Write this sentence on the board:

    Henry's stomach growled as he opened his lunch box.

- Read the sentence aloud to the students. *We know the effect. Henry's stomach growled. Stop to talk about the cause.*
- Have the students share the inferred cause. (Henry was hungry).
- *Now try one with an inferred effect.*
- Write this sentence on the board:

    Liz was late getting to the bus stop.

- Read the sentence aloud to the students. *In this sentence we know the cause. If Liz is late to the bus stop, what is the inferred effect? Stop to talk about the effect.*
- Have the students share the inferred effect. (Liz missed the bus.)
- *When the author does not give us the cause and the effect, we can use our knowledge to help us better understand the information.*

Guided Practice - Cause and Effect Inferred

    Materials: Sentences for Inferred Cause and Effect
                   Transparency of Cause and Effect Graphic Organizer (PDR-CD)
                   Teacher selected text for shared reading or read aloud

- *Today as we read sentences there will be opportunities to infer about the cause and effect of an event. Be sure to listen closely so you can make inferences using what you know from the text along with your prior knowledge. When we have finished reading the sentences, we will write down our thoughts.*
- Read the sentences. Stop after reading each sentence. Allow the students to stop to talk about inferred causes or inferred effects.
- Guide the students if needed. Ask students to share their thinking and explain how they made that inference.
- When you have completed the sentences, show the graphic organizer to them.
- *Let's write what we have learned on this graphic organizer. This will help us remember what we read and to better understand the story.*
- Complete the graphic organizer with the class. Use think aloud talk as you guide them in completing the information.
- *We have practiced with inferred cause and effect. I want you to use what you have learned as you read from day to day. It will help you better understand what you are reading.*

Independent Practice - Cause and Effect Inferred

Read Aloud and Shared Reading

- Students practice finding the inferred cause and effect during read aloud and shared reading. Use stopping points and ask student to turn to their partner and discuss their inferred cause or effect.

Small Group Reading

Materials: Text used in small group
Cause and Effect Graphic Organizer

- Ask students reread the book they are reading during small reading group.
- Teacher and students work together to complete the cause and effect graphic organizer.

Independent Reading

Materials: Texts on independent reading levels
Student response journals

- Ask students to read a text on their independent reading level. After reading ask students to write the cause or effect that is stated in the story in their student response journals.
- Ask students to draw or write the inferred cause or effect in their student response journals..

A Step Beyond

- Ask students to find the cause and effect when reading independently. They share the cause with a partner and the partner states the effect. Or they may share the effect and the partner states the cause.
- Provide a station to practice cause and effect. Provide a card with a stated 'cause' and ask students to draw or write possible effects.
- Students draw or write about something that happened to them. and then identify the cause and the effect.
- Provide a station with causes and effects picture cards or written examples on index cards. The students must match the cause with the correct effect.

Cause and Effect
Across the Curriculum

Math	• Addition/Subtraction • If you add, then you have more • If you subtract, then you have less
Science	• Discuss cause and effect with units of study (magnets, light, sound, etc.) • Safety • Animal Covering
Social Studies	• Historical events • Needs and Wants
Other	• School Rules • Art: adding 2 colors to make a new color • Music: playing instruments

Comparing Story Variants

Comparing Story Variants

Teacher Talk

What: (What is Comparing Story Variants?) In order to have a deeper understanding of stories, first, it is important to notice how story details are alike and then notice how they are different. Things you can compare in stories are: the plot, setting, characters, problem, theme, and solution.

Why: (Why does it help you as a reader?) When the reader compares story variants, they are able to make connections between the stories and understand the stories better.

When: (When is it used during reading?) Readers use this strategy after they have read one or more stories.

What does research tell us about this strategy?

Good readers "draw from, compare, and intergrate their prior knowledge with material in the text." Duke, Nell K. and Pearson P. David (2002). *Effectice Practices for Developing Reading Comprehension.* Scholastic Red

What is expected at this level when using the strategy?

Students at this level compare stories in print to plays, and compare characters, setting, and events.

What prior knowledge or schema do the students need to have?

The students must be familiar with the story elements that will be compared, such as setting, characters, problem, and resolution. They must remember details about the variables to be compared for likenesses and differences. If more than one story is used, the students need to be knowledgeable of them both.

What are cautions and tips when introducing this strategy?

- Start with one story and one variable. Gradually move to two stories with one variable.

- Students must understand the meaning of characters, setting, story problem, and resolution before they can compare them to one another.

- Students need to understand character traits in order to successfully compare two characters.

- It is generally easier for young students to compare characters and settings before problems and resolutions.

- When using two different texts to compare story problems or resolutions, be sure they are clear enough for the students to grasp.

Expectations

Comparing Story Variants – One Story			
Strategy Introduced – I **Strategy Developed – D**	**K**	**1**	**2**
Reading	I	I	D
Writing			

Comparing Story Variants – Two Stories			
Strategy Introduced – I **Strategy Developed – D**	**K**	**1**	**2**
Reading		I	D
Writing			

Comparing Story Variants

Introduction

Materials: Comparing Story Variants Definition Chart

- Prepare and display a Comparing Story Variants Definition Chart like the one shown below. A blackline master is also provided on the PDR-CD. The teacher should enlarge the chart, create their own example of the chart, or make a transparency to show the students.

- Use the definition chart to introduce the strategy. Discuss the name of and definition of the strategy, including why and when to use the strategy during reading. (Refer to Teacher Talk)

Comparing Story Variants

Comparing how things are alike and different helps readers better understand the story. Readers compare the:

- Setting
- Characters
- Problems
- Resolutions

Key Phrases to Focus Talk
- _____ and _____ were alike because_____.
- _____ and _____ were different because _____.

- When discussing the definition and key phrases use an example of a situation or familiar book to activate prior knowledge about the strategy prediction.

Model

Materials: Comparing Story Variants Definition Chart
Pictures of two different characters to compare

- Display and review the Comparing Story Variants Definition Chart. Think aloud and explain the definition to the students. Use pictures from familiar books to illustrate the definition.

- *Our definition tells us that if we compare two characters, we can better understand them. I think I will give it a try.* Display the pictures of two characters you chose to compare.

- *I am going to look closely at these two characters to see how they are alike and how they are different.* Think aloud to discuss the two characters. Include appearance, facial expressions, type of clothing, activities they are shown doing, setting, anything that gives you clues about each character.

- *After looking at the two characters closely, I see ways they are alike and different. I know more about each of the characters.*

- Ask students stop to talk about the characters of the two stories.
- ***Now I want you to think of other ways the two characters in the story are alike or different. Turn to your partner and say, _____ and _____ were _____ because _____.***
- Allow students enough time to share their thinking with their partner. Ask several students to share their thinking and discuss.
- **Note:** Use the lesson format above to compare settings, problems, and resolution of stories. Kindergarten and first grade students will be comparing characters and setting. Comparing problems and resolutions is a more advanced skill and should be modeled and practiced with teacher support.

Activity 1

Materials: Comparing Story Variant Definition Chart
Text with two different characters to compare

- ***We have learned about character traits and how they help us understand the character and what is happening in the story. I wonder if when there are two characters in the story, it will help me understand the story better when I compare the two characters.***
- Review the Comparing Story Variant Definition Chart.
- Display the texts you selected to comparing.
- ***I think that as I read today I will focus on the characters _____ and _____. When I am finished, I will see if comparing these two characters helped me understand the story better.***
- Read the story. Think aloud to compare the two characters as you read. Use the key phrases to model at the pre-selected stopping points to compare how they are alike and different.
- ***Reading the story and I thinking about how the characters are alike and different, help me understand the story better.***
- Ask the students stop to talk about the characters of the two stories.
- ***Now I want you to give it a try. Turn to your partner and say, _____ and _____ are _____(alike or different) because _____.***
- Allow students enough time to share their thinking with their partner. Ask several students to share their thinking and discuss how it helped them to understand the characters and the story better.
- **Note:** Use the lesson format above to compare settings, problems and resolution of stories.

Activity 2

Materials: Comparing Story Variants Definition Chart
Comparing Variants Venn Diagram Organizer (PDR-CD)

- **Note:** This lesson is longer, but very important. For younger readers this lesson can be done in two sessions. Compare the differences of the story in one lesson and the ways they are alike as another.

- *Now I know that comparing two characters in a story helps me better understand the story. Today I will compare the setting using two different stories. I am going to compare the setting in the stories of <u>The Little Red Hen</u> and <u>Little Red Riding Hood.</u>*

- *Since I am comparing the settings of two different stories, I going to use a graphic organizer or Venn diagram to help organize my thoughts.*

- Prepare and display the Venn diagram as a transparency or enlarged on a chart. Fill in the words Settings in the appropriate blank.

- Write Little Hen above the first circle. *I will write my thoughts about Little Red Hen in this circle.*

- Write Little Red Riding Hood above the second circle. *I will write my thoughts about Little Red Riding Hood in this circle.*

- *I am going to start with Little Red Hen. I know the story happened on a farm. I know there was a hen, a dog, a cat, and a duck. I also know there was wheat on the farm because that is what Little Red Hen used to make her bread. I know there was a house with a kitchen in which she cooked her bread. I also know that the story took place in the daytime.* Write your thoughts on the Venn diagram as you think aloud.

- *Now I am going to think about Little Red Riding Hood. I know the story happened in the woods. There were large trees in the woods. I know the characters were Little Red Riding Hood, her grandmother, the wolf and the woodcutter. I know there was a Grandmother's house. I also know it happened during the day.*

- Write your thoughts on the Venn diagram as you think aloud. Continue to use think aloud and compare how the settings are different.

- *Now that I know how the settings were different, I think I will look at each of the settings and see how they were alike.*

- Write in the middle circle of the Venn diagram as you compare how the stories are alike.

- *I can look at my diagram and see that each of the stories had animals in them. I can also see that both stories had plants. One had wheat and the other had tall trees. Both stories had houses in them. Both of the stories happened in the daytime.*

- *Now that I have gathered my thoughts about the settings of both stories, I will see if the settings help me understand the stories better. One had farm animals and the other had forest animals.*

- *I think the forest setting was important in Little Red Riding Hood because the animal that tricked her was a wolf. I do not think that farm animals would have tricked Little Red Riding Hood.*

- *The forest would be a scary place to me because the wolf would scare me, but the hen, dog, cat, and duck in <u>The Little Red Hen</u> would not.*

- *The settings help me realize one story happens in a safe place and the other happens in a scary place. In <u>Little Red Riding Hood</u>, the setting helps me know that something is going to happen to Little Red Riding Hood and that she might be in danger.*

- *I can also see from my diagram that each story has plants in them. Once again I think that helps me understand the stories better.*

- *The hen needed the wheat in order to make bread. The wolf would have had trouble hiding from Little Red Riding Hood if there had not been lots of trees. He would have had trouble hiding behind a bundle of wheat.*

- *The houses were also important to each story. The Little Red Hen could not have made bread without her kitchen tools and oven. Grandma's house was important because that is where Little Red Riding Hood was headed to visit. The wolf needed to use the house to disguise himself as Grandma in her bed. Little Red Riding Hood was familiar with Grandma's house and thought nothing about going inside of it.*

- *Both of the stories also happen during the day. This is important because of the events in both stories. The farm animals in the story would sleep mostly at night and work during the day. Little Red Riding Hood also would have been asleep in bed at night.*

- *I have really learned a lot about the two stories and why the setting of each was so important. Comparing the settings of the two stories really does help in understanding the stories better.*

- Ask the students to stop to talk about the settings of the two stories.

- *Now I want you to think about some other ways the two settings in the story are alike or different. Turn to your partner and say, _____ and _____ were _____ _ because _____.*

- Allow students enough time to share their thinking with their partner. Ask several students to share their thinking and discuss how it helped them to understand the story better.

Guided Practice

Activity 1

Large Group Reading

> Materials: Fables: <u>The Tortoise and the Hare</u> and <u>The Crow and the Pitcher</u>
> Compare Organizer (PDR-CD)

- *We have learned that comparing how things are alike and different in stories help us to better understand the stories.*

- *Today we are going to compare the resolutions of two fables. We will review and listen to the fables and then talk about how the resolutions were alike and different.*

- *The first fable we will use is <u>The Tortoise and the Hare.</u> Many of you already know this fable but listen as I read it aloud.*

- Read the fable aloud to the students. Ask students to **stop to talk** about the problem and resolution.

- *Now I want you to think about the problem and resolution in the story. Turn to your partner and say, I think the problem and resolution in the story was _____.* Allow students enough time to share their thinking with their partner. Allow several students to share their thinking.

- *Today you are going to organize your thoughts about the problem and resolution of both fables.*

- **Options:** 1. Prepare the Compare Organizer with the names of the fables preprinted on each section. 2. Guide students in preparing the Compare Organizer if students are capable of labeling it themselves.

- On the top of the front left flap have them write <u>The Tortoise and the Hare.</u> On the top front right flap, have them write <u>The Crow and the Pitcher</u>. Under each of the two titles, have the students draw or write the problem in the fable. Have the students open up their Compare organizer. Inside the left flap have the students draw or write the resolution of the problem for the tortoise. Inside the right flap, have the students write the resolution for the crow.

- On the inside middle of the student graphic organizer, have the students share how the resolution of both stories were similar. This would also be the common moral of each story. (The tortoise and the crow kept working until they got what they wanted. Neither of them gave up.)

- Ask the students stop to talk as they share their organizers with one another.

- *Now I want you to turn and talk to your partner and say, The problem in _____ was _____ and it was resolved by _____.*

- Allow students enough time to share their thinking with their partner. Ask several students to share their thinking and discuss how it helped them to understand the story better.

Small Group Reading

        Materials: Texts used in small group
                    Comparing Story Variants Venn Diagram (PDR-CD / optional)
                    Compare Organizer (PDR-CD / optional)
                    Student response journals

- After small group or guided reading lesson, ask students use their book(s) to compare two story variants. Students stop to talk to their partner and compare story variants using key phrases to start their talk. They may compare characters, settings, problems, or resolutions.

- **Options:** Modify the activity and use this as a time for the teacher to name the strategy and model for students during small group.

- **Options:** 1. Students draw or write their information on a Venn diagram or Compare Organizer. 2. Students draw or write information and write about their comparisons in their student response journals.

Independent Practice

        Materials: Texts on independent reading levels
                    Compare Organizer (PDR-CD)

- Students read a book on their independent reading level. They choose two characters from the book to compare. Student completes the Compare Organizer to show his thinking.

A Step Beyond

- Remember kindergarten and first grade students will be mostly comparing characters and settings. Students, who are capable, may compare story problems and resolutions.

- Provide a station with books for the students to explore and discuss different characters, settings, story problems, and resolutions.

- Using a book series, have the students compare story variants. Allow the students to choose a graphic organizer of their choice to use in organizing their thoughts. (Book series may include Toad and Frog, Arthur, Nate the Great, etc.)

- Provide the student with a list of fairy tales. Have them choose two and compare one of the story variants.

- Students compare how characters and settings change over time.

Comparing Story Variants
Across the Curriculum

Math	• **Compare addition to subtraction** • **Compare 2 numbers** • **Compare units of time or measurement**
Science	• **Compare "setting" of two different locations (landforms, etc.)** • **Compare 2 states of matter (liquid/solid)**
Social Studies	• **Compare "setting" of two different locations (people, customs)** • **Compare 2 historical figures (Washington and Lincoln)**
Other	• **Brainstorm and list songs that have the same setting or characters: (Little Bunny Foo Foo/Here Comes Peter Cottontail; Bingo/Old McDonald Had a Farm)** • **Compare the setting of two art prints.**

Author's Craft

Author's Purpose

Author's Purpose

Teacher Talk

What: (What is author's purpose?): the author has a reason or purpose for writing. In order to make an impression, he presents the reader with a message or an idea. When you start to read, try to figure out the author's purpose. It will help you in tow ways: you will have a better understanding of the message, and you will be able to decide if the author was able to do what he set out to do.

Why: (Why does it help you as a reader?): If we understand the purpose, we can better understand what the author wrote. You understand why you are reading.

When: (When do you use it during reading?) ? If you understand why the author wrote, you can better understand what he/she has written.

What does research tell us about this strategy?

Research by Duke and Kays (1998) states, "It is important for young readers to read expository material." Kays, J., & Duke, N. K. (1998).
Getting students into information books. *Teaching PreK-8, 29*(2), 52-54.

What is expected at this level when using the strategy?

Kindergarten and first graders can differentiate texts for entertainment and informative text. It is important that both types of texts be use in these classrooms.

What prior knowledge or schema do the students need to have?

The child who heard many books read will probably master this strategy quickly. Kindergarten and first grade will need repeated modeling and practice with informative texts.

What are the cautions and tips when introducing this strategy?

•   Most expository texts are read differently than narrative texts. They may share information through graphs, tables, etc. Students need to know how to use these types of illustrations.

•   Students need to know the difference between "information" and "story elements".

•   There should be a balance between narrative and expository reading. Some students prefer one over the other.

•   Some texts may be both narrative and expository. Discuss which parts of the text are narratives and which are expository. Example: Magic School Bus series.

Expectations

Author's Purpose			
Grade Introduced – I **Grade Developed – D**	**K**	**1**	**2**
Reading	I	D	D
Writing		I	D

Author's Purpose

Introduction

Materials: Author's Purpose Definition Chart

- Prepare and display the Author's Purpose Definition Chart like the one shown below. A blackline master is also provided on PDR-CD. The teacher should enlarge the chart, create their own example of the chart, or make a transparency to show the students.

- Use the definition chart to introduce the strategy. Discuss the name of and definition of the strategy, including why and when to use the strategy during reading. (Refer to Teacher Talk)

Author's Purpose
An author writes to...

Entertain	**Give Information**

- When discussing the definition and key phrases use an example of a situation or familiar book to activate prior knowledge about the strategy prediction.

Model

Materials: Author's Purpose Definition Chart
Teacher Selected Text (narrative and expository)

- Use the same lesson format to teach each lesson. One lesson will model the narrative text and the other will model the expository text.

- The author may have more than one purpose and may combine types of writing to share his message. For modeling purposes use a book that has only one purpose.

Narrative Text:

- Review the Author's Purpose Definition Chart with the students.

- ***Today I am going to read a book. After I read the book I will see if I think the author wrote the book to entertain me or to inform me.***

- Introduce the book to be read aloud. Share the cover and some of the pictures. Use think aloud to talk about why you think the book is a narrative. ***I notice that there are characters in the story and the pictures tell me the characters are doing something. I see there are quotation marks that indicate there is a*** *conversation. Let's read the book and I will decide if I am correct.*

- Read the book.
- *I think the author did write this story to entertain. I enjoyed what happened and was anxious to find out what might happen next. This story was written to entertain me. This kind of story is called a narrative.*
- Allow time for the students' to stop to talk. They are to share a book that they have heard or read in which the author's purpose was to entertain. How did they know?

Expository Text:

- Review the Author's Purpose Definition Chart with the students.
- *I read a book and found out the author wrote it to entertain me. It had interesting characters and I enjoyed reading to find out what would happen and how it would end.*
- *Today, I will read a different book. I am going to see if the author's purpose is to entertain or inform. I see a lot of pictures of _____.*
- Introduce the book to be read aloud. Use think aloud to talk about why you think the story may be expository. *There does not seem to be animals or people talking and doing things that I usually see in a story. I see some charts. I believe this book will inform me. Listen closely and I will decide if I am correct.*
- Read the book aloud.
- *I think the author did write to inform me. I now know a lot about _____. I learned _____.*
- *This is an expository text. The author wrote to inform me.*
- Allow the students to stop and talk. Have them share a book they have read or heard in which the author's purpose was to inform. How did they know?

Guided Practice

Materials: Teacher selected texts (narrative and expository)

- This activity should be taught at least two times. Once using a narrative text and once using an expository text.
- *We have learned that an author can write to entertain or inform. Today we will read a story together. It will be your job to tell me the purpose for which the author wrote.*
- Guide the students in looking at the book before you begin reading. *Are there clues about if the text is a narrative or expository text?*
- Read the book aloud or together as shared reading. During the reading of the book, stop to talk about their thinking.
- *Now that we have read the book, stop to talk to your partner. Is it a narrative written to entertain or an expository written to inform? Explain your thinking.*

- ***The book is a ___. It was written by the author to ___.***

Shared Reading

Materials: Teacher selected texts (narrative and expository)

- Read the text together
- The students decide if it is a narrative or expository text.
- Allow the students to stop to talk and provide evidence to prove their response.

Small Group Reading

Materials: Texts used in small groups
Student response journals

- Students reread texts from small group.
- Have the students write the name of each text in their student response journal. Next to each title, the student will write Narrative or Expository and write a sentence explaining why, providing evidence from the text to prove their response.

Independent Practice

Activity 1

Materials: Texts on independent reading levels

- The students read two texts.
- Askl students to work with with a partner to discuss the author's purpose and provide evidence to prove their thinking.

Activity 2

Materials: Two boxes – one labeled Narrative/Entertain and the other labeled Expository/Inform
Texts on independent reading levels

- The students read a text on their independent reading level.
- Ask the students to decide the author's purpose, to entertain or to inform.
- Then the students place the text in the appropriate box.

A Step Beyond

- During a science or social studies unit, the children can write their own informative texts about what is being studied.
- The children can write narratives about what they did during a holiday or special time. Examples might include a birthday, winter break, vacation, etc. Pictures and

conversation can be included.

Author's Purpose
Across the Curriculum

Math	
Science	After reading an expository text, pair it with a narrative. Example: After reading about magnets, read the book <u>The Magnet Dog</u>
Social Studies	Read an informational text about a famous person or event. Then read an entertaining story about the same person or event. This can tie into a talk about historical fiction.
Other	In art, read information and facts about a painting and then let the students talk about or write a story with the painting as the setting.

Genre Format

Genre Format

Teacher Talk

What: (What is genre format?) Genre Format is the special way authors write their stories to help you understand what they are trying to tell you. Authors can choose formats like fairy tales, poems, stories, newsletters or books with information and facts.

Why: (Why does it help you as a reader?) When you identify the Genre Format it helps you know how to read, understand, and remember what the author is telling you.

When: (When do you use it during reading?) Before you read look at the text and think about how the author is writing their story.

What does research tell us about this strategy?

In a research study published by Nell Duke (2000), it was found that "students must have experience with the types of text we wish them to be able to read and write."

Duke, N.K. (2000). For the rich it's richer: Print experiences and environments offered to children in very low- and very high-socioeconomic status first-grade classrooms. *American Educational Research Journal*, 37,(2), p. 441-478.

What is expected at this level when using the strategy?

Students are introduced to the different genres authors use to share their message. The teacher discusses the features that help readers know the genre of a text. Students practice using the genre of the text to prepare for reading, setting goals before the reading.

What prior knowledge or schema do the students need to have?

Students at this level listen and differentiate between fiction and nonfiction. They also understand simple story structure.

What are the cautions and tips when teaching this strategy?

- Students must have an understanding of fact and fantasy before introducing fiction and nonfiction.
- Students need to recognize the parts of a book, such as cover, title page, and table of contents.
- Students establish a purpose when listening and reading to be entrained, or get information.
- Students are aware of stories and difference forms of nonfiction text such as books with facts, lists, newsletters and signs.

Expectations

Genre Format			
Grade Introduced – I **Grade Developed – D**	**K**	**1**	**2**
Reading	I	D	D
Writing		I	D

Genre Format

Introduction

Materials: Genre Format Definition Chart

- Prepare and display the Genre Format Definition Chart shown below. A blackline master is also provided on the PDR-CD. The teacher should enlarge the chart, create their own example of the chart, or make a transparency to show the students.

- Use the definition chart to introduce the strategy. Name and define the strategy, including why and when to use the strategy during reading. (Refer to Teacher Talk)

- Display a variety of different genre formats using familiar texts, such as a fiction picture book, newspaper, children's magazine, and a non-fiction picture book.

Genre Format

Authors pick the **genre format** that fits what they want to tell you.

| list | sign | news | nonfiction | fiction |

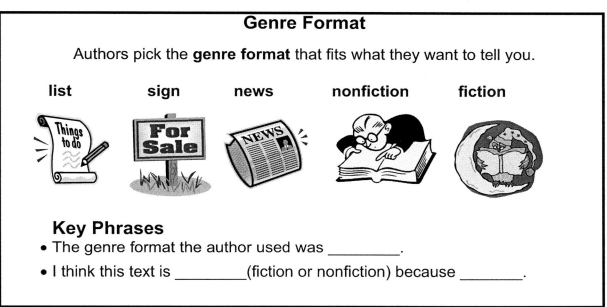

Key Phrases
- The genre format the author used was _____.
- I think this text is _____(fiction or nonfiction) because _____.

Model

Materials: Genre Format Definition Chart
Short texts (1 familiar fiction and non-fiction texts)

- Display the fiction and non-fiction texts for students to view. Review the introduction using the Genre Format Definition Chart.

- Using think aloud model how to look at the text and think aloud about the features you notice to decide if the text is fiction or non-fiction.

- ***We have been talking about how authors write stories different ways depending on what they are trying to tell us. Before I start to read I look at the title, cover and the inside of the book to find out what kind of book I will be reading.***

- Select a fiction text on display. Introduce the title of the book and the author. Think aloud about the illustrations on the cover and the title of the book and make a prediction of what the strategy is going to be about.

- Continue to look through the inside of the book and think aloud about what you notice. Features to point out: illustrations, characters, setting, story about events, etc. Make a prediction about the genre format. Model the key phrase and say, ***I think this is a fiction story_____ because _____.*** Give evidence from the text for your thinking. Point to the word fiction and icons on the definition poster.

- Repeat the same procedure using think aloud to model what you notice when looking at a non-fiction text.

- Continue to look through the inside of the book and think aloud about what you notice. Model the key phrase and say, ***I think this is a nonfiction book because _____.*** Give evidence from the text for your thinking. Point to the word non-fiction and icons on the definition poster.

- Let students give it a try. Choose one more text from the display. Look through the inside of the book and think aloud about what you notice. ***Now, it's your turn to give it a try. Turn to your partner and say, I think this is a _____ (fiction/ non-fiction or point to the poster icons) book. I think this because_____.***

Options: 1. Ask students to bring a book from their book boxes to the floor and use one of their own books to give it a try. They turn to their partner and discuss what they notice and decide the type of genre (fiction or non-fiction). 2. Same as above except the teacher provides texts and partnerships pick one book to use.

Guided Practice

Whole Group or Shared Reading

Materials: Short text (Texts used in Modeling and a familiar non-fiction text)
Genre Format Definition Chart
Display and refer to the two texts used in the previous modeling lesson.

- ***Yesterday we talked about something called Genre Format and we looked at these two books. We talked about how authors use special ways to write depending on what they want to tell you. Sometimes they write stories with characters, settings and sometimes they write true information or facts about topics they want you to know.***

- Remind students of the definition for genre format and review if necessary.

- ***Today, we are going to look at a nonfiction texts called _____. I am going to read and think aloud about what I notice about the genre format as I read. I need everyone to tune in, and I will begin to read.*** The teacher uses think aloud to notice nonfiction features and tell how they help us as readers.

- ***The title of the book is _____. The author of the book is _____. I notice that the book has real pictures of _____ on the cover. As I look through the book I see headings, captions, words in different colors, (name things you see as you quickly look through the book). It looks like the book may be a nonfiction book with facts about _____.***

- *I'm going to read and decide if I think this is a nonfiction story with facts about* _____. Read using **think aloud** to talk about what you see as you read.

- *The picture has a line that points to a word in big bold print and it names what is in the picture. This is important because it tells me the name of the* _____ *in the picture.*

- *I see a chart with information about* _____. *I know these are facts about* _____. Continue to read **thinking aloud** about the nonfiction features you notice. **Think aloud** about the information these features give you and why it is important to read them.

- *Now, I'm going to let you give it a try, turn to your partner and say: I think this is a* _____ *text. I think this because*_____. *Give evidence for your thinking.*

Option: Teacher provides a copy of a nonfiction text for each partnership. Students work with partners to decide if the text is a fiction or nonfiction text and give evidence for their thinking. **Option:** Students can discuss the features they noticed and use their student response journals to write down the features they noticed to prove their thinking.

- As students are ready, model and practice different features of nonfiction text using the lesson above or a Shared Reading Text.

Guided Practice

Small Group

Materials: Sets of non-fiction texts on instructional reading level

- *Early and Emergent Readers -* Teacher introduces title and author of the book for small group practice. Make predictions or ask "I wonder…" questions before reading. Predict if you think it is a fiction or nonfiction text by what you notice about the book.

- Students read entire text orally as the teacher observes and coaches as needed.

- Teacher develops the teaching point(s) from reading and presents to the group.

- At the end of the lesson quickly discuss if the predicts made before reading are correct. Is the book fiction or nonfiction? Students give evidence for their thinking.

Option: If appropriate students can turn to their partner and tell them what they predict before reading and after reading they can turn to their partner and discuss if they were correct and give evidence for their thinking.

Fluent Readers – Reading Silently

- As students reach the Traditional Levels 2-2.5 and read silently ask students to mark stopping points before reading. Students make stopping points by using sticky notes to make where to stop in the text. Stopping points should be small amounts of text where students can practice a strategy. Students read to the stopping point silently and then turn to their partner and practice a strategy using a key phrase given by the teacher. Example: Ask students to mark the first stopping point. Ask students to read to the stopping point and turn to their partner and say "I think this is _____. I think this because …" Students provide evidence to prove their thinking. Teacher listens as students discuss their thinking with partners and reteaches as needed. Students share with the group and discuss evidence. Select the next stopping point and continue.

Independent Practice

Materials: Variety of nonfiction texts, big books, picture books, newsletters
Student response journals, sticky notes
Various graphic organizers

- Students listen to non-fiction text on tape and list or draw the non-fiction features then noticed in their student response journal. Students draw and label information from the text in their student response journal.

- Students reread Shared Reading texts in the Literacy Station. Students use sticky notes to mark pages where they notice non-fiction features and then talk about how these features help them as readers with their partner. Students can share the same text or use two different text and compare.

- Students read non-fiction texts during independent reading. The texts can be new texts or rereading from small group practice. As students read they use their student response journals to list or draw the features of non-fiction they notice.

- Students read non-fiction texts and complete the Share Sheets. Students work with partners to discuss.

- Students work in stations to read non-fiction texts provided and use graphic organizers to list features, the page number and how this feature helps them as a reader.

- Students select several non-fiction texts and work independently or with a partner to list the features they find in their student response journals and compare the texts and decide which provides the most non-fiction features.

A Step Beyond

- Provide short non-fiction texts on a variety of levels and topics. Students select a text and use it to write a short report using the same features of non-fiction.

- Create a bulletin board called, Features of Genre Format. Ask students to look through magazines or newspapers, etc. and bring examples of features of non-fiction text. Label one side of the board Non-fiction and the other side Fiction. Place the samples where they go on the bulletin board. For now students may only bring samples of nonfiction. Leave the board up and when you study fiction have student bring samples to place on board and then compare.

- Use school magazines appropriate for your grade level and discuss how nonfiction features help you as a reader to read and understand the author's message. Discuss why the author would pick this format to tell his information.

- Students work together to create a classroom newsletter. Students are given a topic; they draw pictures and label, illustrate and dictate the story, write and illustrate, or work with a small group to research a topic and write an article for the newsletter. Provide samples of newsletters and encourage students to use features of nonfiction texts.

Genre Format
Across the Curriculum

Math	Use the term fact when talking about math answers.
Science	Discuss the genre used when reading science texts.
Social Studies	Nonfiction biographies
Other	Drama: Act out a fantasy story Library: Locating a fiction and non-fiction book

Fact and Fantasy

Fact and Fantasy

Teacher Talk

What: (What is fact and fantasy?) A <u>fact</u> is something you know is true.

<u>Fantasy</u> is something you know is not true. It is imaginary or make believe.

Why: (Why does it help you as a reader?) It is important for the reader to know when they are reading to gain knowledge and when reading is entertainment.

When: (When is it used during reading?) Readers use <u>fact</u> and <u>fantasy</u> when determining if characters and events are real or imaginary. Recognizing fact from fantasy helps the reader set a goal or purpose for reading.

What does research tell us about this strategy?

In a research study published by Nell Duke (2000), it was found that "students must have experience with the types of text we wish them to be able to read and write."

Duke, N.K. (2000). For the rich it's richer: Print experiences and environments offered to children in very low- and very high-socioeconomic status first-grade classrooms. *American Educational Research Journal*, 37,(2), p. 441-478.

What is expected at this level when using this strategy?

Students begin to determine a reason or purpose before reading exploring factual and fantasy features during read alouds, shared reading, guided and independent reading. Readers talk about the goal for reading, thinking about the author's purpose and how they will read the text.

What prior knowledge or schema do the students need to have?

Students need an understanding of real and make believe. Fact and fantasy must be taught before fiction and nonfiction.

What are cautions and tips when teaching this strategy?

- We often think that children in elementary school know the difference between facts and fantasy. This is not always the case. Be sure the students have this skill before moving on to fiction and non-fiction.

- When discussing fact and fantasy, start with things the students are familiar with such as dragons, fairies, etc.

- Caution when wording examples for students. For example, if you say to the students "I can fly." Most will say it is make believe, but there may be the one who says fact. He will picture you flying in an airplane.

Expectations

Fact and Fantasy			
Grade Introduced – I Grade Developed – D	K	1	2
Reading	I	D	D
Writing			

Fact and Fantasy

Introduction

Materials: Fact and Fantasy Definitions Chart

- Prepare and display the Fact and Fantasy Definition Chart shown below. A blackline master is also provided at the end of the section. The teacher should enlarge the chart, create their own example of the chart, or make a transparency to show the students.

- Use the definition chart to introduce the strategy. Name and define the strategy, including why and when to use the strategy during reading. (Refer to Teacher Talk)

Fact and Fantasy

A **fact** is something that is true. **Fantasy** is something that is not true. It is imaginary or make believe. It is not logical.

  Fact: Owls live in trees.

  Fantasy: Owls read books.

Key Phrases

- I know this is fact because _____.
- I know this is fantasy because _____.

- When discussing the definition and key phrases use an example of a situation or familiar book to activate prior knowledge about the strategy prediction.

- Use examples of facts and fantasy that are common to their lives to define the fact and fantasy.

Model

Materials: Fact and Fantasy Definitions Chart
Various books including factual pictures and fantasy pictures
Select 3-5 factual pictures and 3-5 fantasy pictures

Fact

- Review the Fact and Fantasy Definitions Chart.
- Preview the books and select 3-5 pictures of factual people or   animals.
- Display 3-5 examples of facts (pictures of people or animals etc.)
- As you discuss facts using the examples above use the key phrase to model. Say, ***If I know a fact is true, then I know it is a fact that _____.*** Repeat the key phrase as you discuss 3-4 examples.
- ***This time, I want you to give it a try.*** Display the last picture of a factual character (an animal, person, etc.). ***Look at the picture. Now turn to your partner and say, I know this is a fact because_____.***
- Allow students time to share their thinking with their partner. Ask several students to share their thinking and discuss.

- **Note:** Model Fantasy – Fact and Fantasy may be introduced and modeled together or at the same time.

Fantasy

- Repeat the activity above using fantasy.
- Preview the fantasy books and locate 3-5 pictures of fantasy people or animals.
- *If I know make believe is not true but in the imagination, I know that it is fantasy that I can grow wings and fly. I also know that a cow doing a ballet dance is fantasy. They are not logical and do not make sense.*
- Model 3-4 examples of facts that are common to their lives (what they are wearing, things they do in the classroom, pictures of people or animals etc.)
- As you discuss fantasy using the examples above use the key phrase to model. Say, *If I know make believe is fantasy, then I know it is fantasy that _____.* Repeat the key phrase as you discuss each example.
- *This time, I want you to give it a try.* Display the last picture of make believe characters.
- *Look at the picture. Now turn to your partner and say, I know this is fantasy because_____.*
- Allow students time to share their thinking with their partner. Ask several students to share their thinking and discuss.

Guided Practice

Activity 1

    Materials: Fact and Fantasy Definition Chart
                4 pictures showing fact and 4 pictures showing fantasy
                Student response journals

- Review the Fact and Fantasy Definition Chart. Write fact and fantasy on the board.
- Use think aloud to model for the students. Look at each picture and think aloud describing how you know it is a fact or fantasy. Provide evidence for your thinking. As you make a decision for each picture, place it on the board under the appropriate heading.
- *This time, I want you to give it a try.* Display a picture of make believe characters. *Look at the picture. Now turn to your partner and say, I know this is fantasy because_____.*
- Allow students time to share their thinking with their partner. Ask several students to share their thinking and discuss.
- Ask students to use their student response journals and write the word fact on one side of their paper and fantasy on the other side of their paper. Have them draw an example of each under the term.

Activity 2

> Materials: Fact and Fantasy Definition Chart
> 2 books (1 example of fact and 1 fantasy)

Option: This lesson can be taught over two days, fact and then fantasy.

- Review fact and fantasy definitions using the definition chart.

- Tell the students you want them to think about what they know about fact and fantasy. Remind them of some of the pictures used in the last lesson.

- Explain to them that fact and fantasy can be also found in the words of a story.

- Ask students to tune in as you read aloud and model how you know facts and fantasy. Read aloud 3-5 pre-selected text and stop at stopping points to model your thinking. Use key phrases as you model, *I know these words are facts because _____.*

Option: Fantasy Text is day two of a two-day plan.

- Read the fantasy text and stop at 3-5 pre-selected stopping points to model how you know stories that are make believe. *I know these words are fantasy because _____. They are not logical. I know now that words can also give me clues and let me know if a story is true or if it is just fantasy.*

- *This time I want you to give it a try. I am going to read a few sentences. You will decide if they are facts or make believe.*

- *It was a beautiful spring day. Molly got on her bike to go to her friend's house. On the way she saw a unicorn sitting in the sun. She heard the roar of a dinosaur as she pulled up in front of her friend's house. She rang the doorbell and a two-headed monster answered door. The monster let her in and she went to play with her friend.*

- *Now I want you to stop to talk about fact and fantasy. Turn to your partner and say, I know these words are _____, because_____.*

- Allow students just enough time to share their thinking with their partner. Ask several students to share their thinking and discuss.

Activity 3

> Materials: Fact and Fantasy Definition Chart
> Fact and Fantasy Response Cards

- *For the last few days we have been talking about fact and fantasy. Today we are going to practice using this skill. I am going to read a sentence. If the words are facts then hold up the fact card. If the words are make believe, hold up the fantasy card.*

- Read the following sentences aloud one at a time. Have the students hold up the card that they think represents the words you have read.

- *At the circus, I saw an elephant riding on the back of a dog.*

- *I eat lunch with my friend at school.*

- *I learn new songs in music.*

- *Joe flew to Hawaii on the wing of an airplane.*
- *My friend can run as fast as a cheetah.*
- *My mom and dad are older than I.*
- After every student has held up their card, have students **stop and talk** and share why they chose the card they did.
- *Now I want you to about fact and fantasy. Turn to your partner and say, I know these words are _____ , because_____.*
- Allow students time to share their thinking with their partner. Ask several students to share their thinking and discuss.
- The use of the response card will make it easy to assess the students and provide additional teaching if needed.
- *I have learned that when I read a story I can know if it is true or not by deciding if the text is factual or make believe. Turn to your partner and tell them how you know if a story is fact or fantasy.*
- Allow students time to share their thinking with their partner. Ask several students to share their thinking and discuss.

Small Group

> Materials: Texts used in small reading group
> Student response journals

- After small group guided reading lessons discuss whether the book is fact or fantasy.
- *Now I want you to talk about fact and fantasy. Turn to your partner and say, I know this is _____, because_____.*
- Allow students time to share their thinking with their partner. Ask several students to share their thinking and discuss.

Option: This can be done after the reading for independent work. Students write or draw their response in their student response journal. Students bring their student response journal to small group the next day and share.

- Ask students to use the book for small group reading and reread to find a fact or a fantasy in the story.
- Ask the students to make two columns in their response journal. Label one column fact and the other fantasy.
- Ask each student find a fact in the story and write it under the fact column in his or here response journal.
- Ask each student find an example of make believe in the story and write it under the fantasy column in his or her response journal.
- Ask the students share their responses with one another.

A Step Beyond

- Have the students pair up. One says a sentence to the other. The one listening must hold up their correct fact or make believe response card.
- If they are correct then it is their turn to say a sentence and their partner holds up the correct card.
- Ask students' write a sentence that states a fact and one that includes something that is make believe. Have them illustrate both sentences. The teacher may decide to make a fact/fantasy bulletin board and display their work.
- Students may choose to take a story they are familiar with that is factual and turn it into a make-believe story. These could be shared with the class.
- Provide a station with pictures for the students to cut out and glue under the word fact or fantasy.
- Provide a station with pictures of fact or fantasy for students to sort.
- Provide a station with picture books or rereading books for students to sort.

Fact and Fantasy
Across the Curriculum

Math	Use the term fact when talking about math answers.
Science	Use the term fact when discussing science terms that apply.
Social Studies	Nonfiction biographies
Other	Drama: Act out a fantasy story Library: Locating a fiction and non-fiction book

Fiction and Nonfiction

Fiction and Nonfiction

Teacher Talk

What: (What is Fiction and Nonfiction?)

Fiction is created by the imagination. The events did not really happen. These are usually stories to entertain us. **Nonfiction** has the true facts and the events did really happen. These books are usually giving us facts about someone or something.

Why: (Why does it help you as a reader?) It is important for the reader to know when they are reading to gain knowledge and when reading is entertainment. Nonfiction texts help the reader gather information through

words as well as graphs, drawings, diagrams, maps, and other visual forms.

When: (When do you use it during reading?) Readers use <u>fiction</u> and <u>nonfiction</u> to guide them in their <u>purpose</u> for reading. Readers set goals for reading and ask questions such as; Why am I reading this book?, What do I expect to learn?, and How do I read this book?.

What does research tell us about this strategy?

According to researcher G. Wells (1986), "knowledge of the components of both narrative and expository text is part of being fully literate."

Wells, G. (1986). *The meaning makers*. Portsmouth: Heinemann.

What is expected at this level when using the strategy?

Students at this level listen and differentiate between fiction and nonfiction. They also understand simple story structure.

What prior knowledge or schema do the students need to have?

- Students must have an understanding of fact and fantasy before introducing fiction and nonfiction.
- Students need to recognize the parts of a book, such as cover, title page, and table of contents.
- Students establish a purpose when listening and reading to be entrained, or get information.
- Students are aware of stories and difference forms of nonfiction text such as books with facts, lists, newsletters and signs.

What are the cautions and tips when teaching this strategy?

- Some students confuse fiction with nonfiction. They may think that a fiction story is nonfiction because the events really could happen. Explain that texts like this are called realistic fiction. They are stories that could happen but were created in the imagination or mind of the author to entertain.

Expectations

Strategy: Fiction and Nonfiction			
Grade Introduced – I **Grade Developed – D**	**K**	**1**	**2**
Reading	I	D	D
Writing		I	D

Fiction and Nonfiction

Introduction

Materials: Fiction/NonFiction Chart

- Prepare and display the Fiction/Nonfiction Definition Chart shown below. A blackline master is also provided at the end of the section. Teachers should enlarge the chart, create their own example of the chart, or make a transparency to show the students.

- Use the definition chart to introduce the strategy. Name and define the strategy, including why and when to use the strategy during reading. (Refer to Teacher Talk)

Fiction and Nonfiction

A **fiction** story is created by the imagination and written to entertain us.

A **non-fiction** story has true facts and events and is written to inform us about someone or something.

Key Phrases

- I know this is fiction because _____.
- I know this is non-fiction because _____.

- When discussing the definition and key phrases use an example of a situation or familiar book to activate prior knowledge about the strategy prediction.

- *These remind me of fact and fantasy. Fantasy is not true and fiction books are not true. Facts are true and nonfiction books are true facts*

Model

Activity 1

Materials: Fiction/Nonfiction Definitions Chart
3-5 familiar fiction and nonfiction books

- Review the Fiction/Nonfiction Definition Chart

- Use think aloud to model examples of familiar fiction and nonfiction texts and how you know it is fiction and nonfiction.

- *I am thinking about the story <u>The Three Little Pigs</u>. I know that pigs do not really build houses. I think that story is a fiction story.*

- *Now I am thinking about a story I read about George Washington and how he becomes the first president of the United States. I think that story must be nonfiction because it is full of facts.*

- *It is important for me to know if the book I am reading is fiction or nonfiction. It will help me better understand what I am reading.*

- ***Now I want you to give it a try. Turn to your partner and say, I think the book <u>Cinderella</u> is fiction or nonfiction, because_____.***
- Allow students enough time to share their thinking with their partner. Ask several students to share their thinking and discuss.
- ***Now I want you to think of a book called <u>The Earth and What It is Made Of.</u> Turn to your partner and say, I think the book <u>The Earth and What it is Made Of</u> is fiction or nonfiction, because_____.***
- Allow students enough time to share their thinking with their partner. Ask several students to share their thinking and discuss.

Activity 2

    Materials: Fiction/NonFiction Definitions Chart
                 6 various fiction and nonfiction books (three of each)

- Review the fiction/nonfiction definition using the Chart.
- Tell the students that today you are going to look through some books and decide if they are fiction or nonfiction.
- Share one of the books. Look at the pictures and possibly read a short part of the text. Use think aloud talk as you look at the book. Tell if it is a fiction or nonfiction book and give evidence for your thinking.
- Share 3 of the other books you gathered and model in the same way.
- ***Now I want you to try it on your own.*** Share one of the remaining books. ***Turn to your partner and say, I think the book _____ is fiction or nonfiction, because_____.***
- Allow students enough time to share their thinking with their partner. Ask several students to share their thinking and discuss.
- Repeat the activity with the remaining books.

Guided Practice

    Materials: Fiction/Nonfiction Definitions Chart
                 Various fiction and nonfiction books
                 Student response journals

- Review fiction and nonfiction using the definitions chart.
- Share the books with the students. Select books students will be able to determine if it is fiction or nonfiction. The students will select one book.
- Explain to the students that they are to take the book they chose and write or draw about it. They are to tell if it is fiction or nonfiction. They should have evidence to share how they made their decision.
- Allow students time to complete the activity. Ask students to share their thinking with their partner.
- Ask several students to share their books and responses with the class.

Independent Practice

Activity 1

Small Reading Group
Materials: Texts used in small group reding

- Display several books the group has read during small group reading.

- Ask students to select one of the books.

- Ask students browse through the book to determine if it is fiction or nonfiction.

- *Turn to your partner and say, I think the book _____ is fiction or nonfiction, because _____.*

- Allow students enough time to share their thinking with their partner. Ask several students to share their thinking and discuss.

Activity 2
Materials: Various books including fiction and nonfiction
Fiction/Nonfiction Graphic Organizer

- Provide a selection of fiction and nonfiction books for the students to use to complete the Fiction/Nonfiction Graphic Organizer.

- Model how to use the graphic organizer using a familiar text. (This may be done ahead of time in a small group or large group setting.)

- Ask students to select one fiction and one nonfiction text from the selection you have provided.

- Students use the texts to complete the graphic organizer.

Options: 1. Use as a station activity. 2. Students work with partners to complete the activity. 3. Teacher and students work together as a whole group to complete the activity using familiar texts.

A Step Beyond

- Visit the library and locate the fiction and nonfiction books, and magazines.

- Students write down the title or draw a picture of a book they word like to check out.

- Discuss why the books are located in these sections in the library.

- Students think about their favorite author. Does this author write fiction or nonfiction? Have them share their findings with the class. They may discover that some authors write both fiction and nonfiction.

- Students read the summary from a book flap. They use the information and classify it as fiction or nonfiction.

- Students work in stations to sort books and set up a display of books including fiction and nonfiction books.

- Students work together or independently to write and illustrate a fiction or non-fiction book. Students use books and children's magazines as mentor text.
- Students work with a partner and look through non-fiction texts and write or draw what they notice about the format of the text. Examples, maps, charts, bullets, captions, real pictures or illustrations, bold print. Etc.

Fiction and Nonfiction
Across the Curriculum

Math	Decide if a word problem is fiction or nonfiction.
Science	Short non-fiction articles and science text
Social Studies	Nonfiction biographies
Other	Drama: Act out a fantasy story Library: Locating a fiction and nonfiction book

Appendix

Contents of PDR - CD

Instructional Strategy Definitions Charts, Icons, Activities, Graphic Organizers and Titles for Instruction

Procedural Definition
Getting Ready to Read
Working in Stations
Talking About Your Reading
Where and How to Sit During Reading Time
"Tune In" During Read Aloud
Working as a Community
Reading With a Partner
How to Share – With a Partner
How to Share – With a Group

Key Cognitive Strategy
Predict
Connec
Describe
Ask
Reread
Define
Retell
Summary

Vocabulary Strategy

Context Clues
Graphic Organizer

Synonyms / Antonyms
A Trip to the Zoo
Word Cards
Word Cards
Word Cards
Activity Sheet
Make a Flip Book
Graphic Organizer(s)

Base Word
Base Word Cards – Suffixes
Base Word Cards - Suffixes
Base Word Cards- Suffixes

Best Definition / Beginning Glossary or Dictionary
Make an Animal Dictionary
Graphic Organizer(s)

Story Structure

Main Idea / Supporting Details J
Jack and Jill
The Itsy Bitsy Spider
Jack be Nimble
Little Bo Peep
Hey Diddle Diddle
Graphic Organizer(s)

Setting
Settings (Created by Text Paragraphs)
What is the Setting?
Settings: Same and Different
Graphic Organizer(s)

Character Traits / Emotions / Motives
Graphic Organizer(s)

Plot / Story Problem / Resolution
Do You Know the Whole Story?
Graphic Organizer(s)

Order of Important Events / Sequence
A Weekend at Grandma's House
Activity Cards
Graphic Organizer(s)

Summary
Draw and Write a Summary of the Story
Graphic Organizer(s)

Comprehension

Text to Support Meaning
Jill's Birthday Surprise
I Can Support My Thinking
Graphic Organizer(s)

Inferences (Predictions / Drawing Conclusions)
Graphic Organizer(s)

Cause and Effect
Activity Cards
Cause and Effect Literal Sentences
Cause and Effect Inferred Sentences
Graphic Organizer(s)

Comparing Story Variants
The Crow and the Pitcher
The Tortoise and the Hare
Making a Flip Book
Graphic Organizer(s)

Author's Craft
Author's Purpose

Genre Format
Features of Books
Birthday Invitation
My Summer Vacation
Letter to Mike
Graphic Organizer(s)

Fact / Fantasy
Graphic Organizer(s)

Fiction / Nonfiction
Fiction and Non-fiction Books I Have Read
Graphic Organizer(s)

Discussion Wheels
Mini-lesson planing form(s)
Strategy lesson form(s)
AEA's Five Day Plan

Titles for Instruction